Eurocentrism in Translation Studies

Benjamins Current Topics

Special issues of established journals tend to circulate within the orbit of the subscribers of those journals. For the Benjamins Current Topics series a number of special issues of various journals have been selected containing salient topics of research with the aim of finding new audiences for topically interesting material, bringing such material to a wider readership in book format.

For an overview of all books published in this series, please see
http://benjamins.com/catalog/bct

Volume 54

Eurocentrism in Translation Studies
Edited by Luc van Doorslaer and Peter Flynn

These materials were previously published in *Translation and Interpreting Studies* 6:2 (2011)

Eurocentrism in Translation Studies

Edited by

Luc van Doorslaer
CETRA, University of Leuven / Stellenbosch University

Peter Flynn
CETRA, University of Leuven

John Benjamins Publishing Company
Amsterdam / Philadelphia

The paper used in this publication meets the minimum requirements of
the American National Standard for Information Sciences – Permanence
of Paper for Printed Library Materials, ANSI z39.48-1984.

Library of Congress Cataloging-in-Publication Data

Eurocentrism in Translation Studies / Edited by Luc van Doorslaer and Peter Flynn.

p. cm. (Benjamins Current Topics, ISSN 1874-0081 ; v. 54)

Includes bibliographical references and index.

1. Translating and interpreting--Study and teaching. 2. Eurocentrism. I. Doorslaer,
    Luc van, 1964- editor of compilation. II. Flynn, Peter (Translator), editor of
    compilation.

P306.5.E97   2013

418'.02071--dc23   2013016434

ISBN 978 90 272 0273 4   (Hb ; alk. paper)

ISBN 978 90 272 7163 1   (Eb)

John Benjamins Publishing Co. · P.O. Box 36224 · 1020 ME Amsterdam · The Netherlands

John Benjamins North America · P.O. Box 27519 · Philadelphia PA 19118-0519 · USA

Table of contents

On constructing continental views on translation studies

An introduction

Peter Flynn and Luc van Doorslaer

The articles collected in this volume tackle various aspects of a debate on Eurocentrism in translation studies both in general and in relation to the Americas. The debate emerged during a one-day conference in Antwerp, Belgium on December 2, 2009. The title of the conference, "The Construction of Translation Studies through Translation: Contrasting Various 'Continental' Perspectives" was perhaps more controversial than we realized at the time of its formulation. The scare quotes in 'continental' were meant to express a degree of caution as to the existence of specifically continental perspectives while also being designed to promote debate on any possible differences in perspective emerging from scholarly work from various parts of the world. Rather ambitious for a one-day conference, one might think. The title also contained a teaser in suggesting that translation studies emerged from translation. While this may seem like overstating the obvious to many, it also served in part as a gesture in the direction of Edwin Gentzler's book, *Translation and Identity in the Americas: New Directions in Translation Theory* (Gentzler 2008), which was the main pretext for the conference. As the book indeed discusses many (new and not so new) conceptualizations of translation formulated by translators and writers, the gesture was not out of place. The gesture hence remains valid and extends beyond Gentzler's book in formulating an ongoing question about the relation between translation practices and how they are conceptualized in various languages in various places in the world.

All of the contributors who submitted work were present at the conference and have further developed their arguments in relation to the theme at hand: one of the unpredictable upshots of many a conference whereby a sub-theme ends up being the center of discussion and indeed the topic of this volume. It must be stressed, however, that, although Gentzler's use of the term Eurocentrism, particularly in the context of translation studies in the Americas, did trigger the debate, it was clear from the discussions during the conference that Eurocentrism, or more specifically what was understood by it in translation studies, was far from clear and indeed required further explication. Although similar debates on this theme have been conducted in other disciplines to varying degrees of closure (for instance Shohat & Stam 1994 in media studies), it was thought important to examine how the concept was mobilized and entextualized in the discourse of translation scholars (see van Doorslaer 2010 for an initial exploration). It is obvious to the editors that these contributions will in no way exhaust the debate, the hope being that other collections might follow or that others will pick up where we leave off and continue the discussion.

All of the papers presented here can be considered to varying degrees as discussion papers in that they examine a particular issue or concept either by presenting an overview of its use and how it is understood by scholars or by presenting data to illustrate that use or other possible uses within the field. As Gentzler's book triggered the debate on Eurocentrism (in the Americas) it seems only correct that he be allowed to present his arguments first before we move on to the other contributors. Although they have used Gentzler's book as a touchstone, their papers move beyond it in tackling the work of other authors in order to present a particular stance on the topic or to highlight a given aspect of the debate.

In what follows an attempt will be made to highlight and tie together some of the more salient points emerging from the various papers in relation to the central theme of this volume. Eurocentrism as it is understood in translation studies brings with it a whole set of related terms which further articulate and mobilize the term in various ways. These terms comprise the very definitions or conceptualizations of translation itself and the ways in which these definitions and conceptualizations have reflected and perpetuated particular mindsets through history to the present day (viz. Gentzler's, Valdeón's article in this issue). These mindsets often build on antagonistic views of language, nation and culture, some of which are considered to be out of step with recent developments, particularly the globalization of information flows and the growth of virtual communities for example.

In echoing the title of Mary Snell-Hornby's and Michael Cronin's work, **Edwin Gentzler**'s contribution "Macro- and Micro-Turns in Translation Studies," examines older and more recent turns in translation studies including those in the Americas. At a macro-level Gentzler first contrasts what he terms European (even Eurocentric) definitions of translation with those found in China, India, and the Arab world. He argues that these non-European definitions conceptualize translation in innovative ways that merit closer examination. He argues for a "both/and" approach in putting forward more flexible conceptualizations and definitions of translation, his central thesis being that translation is more constitutive of culture in the Americas than merely a marker of more obvious cultural and linguistic differences. To illustrate the omnipresence of translation in everyday life, he provides a plethora of examples emerging from and building on translation practices. These examples range from more visible resistant approaches to translation in theater and literature (viz. the use of *joual* in Quebec or "cannibalistic" approaches in Brazil) to the daily use of translation in cities, neighborhoods and families. All of these translation activities play an important role in constructing and maintaining a variety of identities often obscured by monolingual views of nation. Gentzler also points out how these translation activities were there from the very beginning of colonization and have played a prominent role in defining America perhaps even more so than iconic foundational texts written in English. Given the multilingualism extant in American societies, he "lobbies for new, open, and less prescriptive definitions and models" of translation in order to gain a better understanding of these societies. He advocates "combining approaches — European and non-European" and moving away from formative nation-based definitions of translation.

It would seem to the editors of this volume therefore that narrower formative views on translation that have had a considerable impact in the past are inherently European or perhaps even Eurocentric. This of course begs two basic questions: 1.What is European: a geographical space? an imperialistic mindset? 2. Are European views on translation necessarily narrow and nation-based? Furthermore, even if this were the case at some stage in the past, is this still the case today?

Much of the argumentation against narrower (linguistic) approaches to translation which indeed were developed in Europe in the mid and latter half of the 20th century[1] revolved around a lack of concern for issues of identity, power and other highly important matters regarding the contexts of translation, all of which have since become main focuses for translation scholars. Interestingly, many of these points of criticism regarding linguistics in general and linguistic approaches to translation studies were dealt with quite comprehensively and debunked in an article by Mona Baker back in 2001. In the conclusion to her article she issues a warning, pointing to how, "the narrow debate about linguistics vs. cultural studies is essentially distracting translation scholars from participating in a wider and far more interesting intellectual debate that is going on all around us" (Baker 2001: 18).

Dirk Delabastita's contribution, "Eurocentrism and the Invention of Traditions in Translation Studies," picks up the theme of Eurocentrism and examines it from another angle, breaking the concept down into a set of underlying beliefs and convictions many of which have fuelled European projects of

---

1. But not only in Europe. Vinay & Darbelnet's work (1958), for instance, was highly influential for generations and still continues to be used today. Many are unaware, however, that their work is a product of translation studies in Canada.

empire. He subsequently highlights the blind spots issuing from narrow forms of Eurocentrism over the centuries: "forms of intellectual dogmatism, ethical arrogance ... a failure to take interest in cultural practices outside the Western sphere, etc." He refers then to what he terms the international turn in translation studies and the growing presence of work by non-Western scholars, all of which provides a more culturally balanced approach to the discipline. He situates Gentzler's work within this framework and regards his latest book as posing a powerful challenge to Eurocentrism.

Rather than reviewing the book, however, Delabastita engages with it meta-discursively, framing his article as a case study in writing about translation. In this sense he traces and examines critically a set of "discursive and logical moves" found in Gentzler's writing. He argues that the plethora of examples of different translation practices and conceptualizations throughout the Americas actually come together discursively thereby giving the examples a sort of "pan-American resonance." He further identifies three intertwining storylines that are woven together to construct and propagate a form of common American cultural identity underlying or running throughout the various cultural sites discussed in Gentzler's book: their rejection of (a) an insipid European ethos of passive recreation," (b) "European (symbolic) dominance," and, subsequently, (c) their "refusal to adopt European" models of translation. These storylines come together to construct "a new, specifically American brand of translation theory." The question remains as to whether these generalizations can be traced to other continents or not. Delabastita actually questions the relevance of continent-based theories of translation, being more interested in deriving theories that are flexible enough to face the challenges posed by globalization while still being able to address issues of more local concern. However, all of this does nothing to take away from the quantity of important evidence Gentzler provides in arguing his case for the omnipresence of translation in the Americas. Delabastita's meta-discursive analysis calls to mind the thrust of the debate found in James Clifford and George Marcus's seminal work, *Writing Culture* (1986), but in this case applied to writing translation (theory). It is obviously important to present and promote approaches to translation from all over the world and ensure that they find their way into the literature. A degree of reflexivity is required to heighten our awareness of the ideological entailments involved in how we write up and present case and counter-case in delineating changes in translation studies. Such reflexivity should continue to inform our own research as well as the general debate on writing translation. Delabastita's contribution sheds light on how such awareness can be heightened.

In a related vein, **Peter Flynn**'s article, "How Eurocentric is Europe? Examining Scholars' and Translators' Contributions to Translation Studies — An Ethnographic Perspective," inquires into whether theories and concepts of translation debated in the literature can actually be attributed to a given geographical space, let alone a cultural or regional mindset. The article traces two trajectories of thought in translation, one academic and international, the other emerging from the discourse of lesser known literary translators in the Dutch-speaking regions of Europe. First, if the concept of Western/Eurocentric can be extended to the Americas and beyond that to other parts of the globe where English is a predominant language (see Tymoczko's position paper at the end of this volume), can one not justifiably wonder whether the concept is at all useful, and much like equivalence, which was declared moribund and a more or less empty signifier in the literature, cannot be considered theoretically redundant? Even within the European (sic) debate one can notice references to Euro-American academic exchanges that show preferences for certain scholars above others: Bourdieu or Derrida perhaps. Is this not a sign of the relative redundancy of the concept?

Second, does this debate take into account the many translators who are active below the horizon of academic inquiry and theoretical speculation? The discourse of the translators discussed in the article — albeit European — rarely features in broader debates on the name and nature of translation studies despite the fact that they have earned local respect as translators. This is not to say that they do not hold there own views on the field in which they work or that their views do not deserve consideration both theoretically and from the point of view of practice. All this puts into perspective one aspect of the translator's visibility (*pace* Venuti); which translators are being consulted on whatever theory of translation? This invisible antagonism leads us to the more visible antagonism in Michael Boyden's article.

In "Beyond Eurocentrism? The Challenge of Linguistic Justice Theory to Translation Studies," **Michael Boyden** examines the meaning of Eurocentric in the United States, showing how the term became increasingly equated with dominant white Euro-Americans in contrast to minority cultures, particularly following the civil rights movement in the 1960s. He points to differences between decolonization in former countries of empire and internal colonization in North America and argues, following Koselleck, that the term Eurocentrism has been largely used in the US as an asymmetrical counterpart, in setting off past from present, there from here, one group from the other. He asks, therefore, how we should understand the politics of "beyond," i.e., moving beyond given, natural or unquestioned versions of reality toward a fairer representation of that reality. In this respect, debates conducted in other disciplines in the humanities since the civil rights movements have pushed for equal representation everywhere, including in the literary canon.

In the debate centering on the various uses of Eurocentrism and its impact upon translation studies (Gambier and van Doorslaer, Hermans, Jacquemond, Price, Tymoczko, and Gentzler, among others) one main view emerges — one of reparation ("setting things straight, getting things right"). It seems to the editors, that this is somehow curiously reminiscent of Whorf's defense of Native American languages and cultures in the face of narrow-gauge views on language and culture at the time, without going so far as to take a strict Sapir-Whorfian[2] stance that might posit unbridgeable gaps in translation theory and practice from one culture to the next.

In the face of the debate on identity, upon which such notions as Eurocentric and non-Eurocentric turn, Boyden calls for a revaluation of more instrumental values at stake in translation activities. Citing the example of language and translation issues in Hawaii he points to the dangers of focusing too sharply on identity to the detriment of other aspects on the translational cline, i.e., access to important sources of wellbeing in everyday life mainly negotiated through the medium of English: education, job opportunities, health care, etc. He puts forward the notion of linguistic justice (Weinstock, Pogge and others) as a means of maintaining a balance between important issues of identity and the more "instrumental" yet no less important issues at stake.

Jacobus Marais's contribution, "The Representation of Agents of Translation in (South) Africa: Encountering Gentzler and Madonella," provides the reader with encounters both historical and theoretical within the domain of translation. In a way, it is a fictional representation of those encounters, but one that poses serious questions about directions of inquiry in translation studies and their relevance for emerging approaches to the discipline in South Africa and by extension other parts of the continent. The debate on the formative force of translation in creating (African) identity in a mixed English-European-African context is a central issue in this contribution. Marais creates encounters and a narrative aiming at intra-continental translation in Africa. Central to his argument is the notion of agency in given historical translation situations, which leads to the following question: can one justifiably formulate viable theory without examining what actually happened in situ? In other words does the general discourse of empire and subaltern apply in the no-man's land he explores? Through this example of a continentalization and further dis-localization of discourse, his approach also impacts on the characteristics of the discipline of translation studies and how they might further unfold in Africa.

"On Fictional Turns, Fictionalizing Twists and the Invention of the Americas" is the title of **Roberto Valdeón**'s contribution, in which he invokes the theoretically vague concept of 'Eurocentrism' as used in the Humanities and the Social Sciences. He parallels the invention of the New World with the perception of Europe as a cohesive geopolitical power, as opposed to the existing reality of the complexity of

---

2. Barnard argues that neither Sapir nor Whorf would have agreed with the more absolutist interpretations of linguistic relativism that followed in their wake (Barnard 2000: 108–111).

identities on the Old Continent. His case study on Bartolomé de las Casas and La Malinche is an illustration of how certain negative images of translators and nations can be created. Texts were ideologically manipulated, largely through or as a result of (mis)translation, in order to construct antagonistic national identities within Europe which largely drew for their justification on the atrocities perpetrated by each party in other parts of the globe. In this contribution the role of translation is far less positive than in Gentzler's discussion of the fictional turn.

Luc van Doorslaer's interview article, "(More than) American Prisms on Eurocentrisms," forms an interesting corollary to the debate in the way it engages with the theme with a view to re-establishing a continental balance, as European authors and one African author have contributed to this volume. The interview article gives the floor to three translation studies scholars from the Americas and invites them to reflect on the criticisms voiced in the papers in this issue. Sherry Simon, Judy Wakabayashi and Maria Tymoczko agreed to respond and provided incisive and well-balanced comments on the points of criticism emerging from the papers.

To conclude, we would like to thank all those who have contributed to this volume for their patience and their willingness to face the topic head-on. Thanks are also due to the editor of *TIS* for maintaining an open-minded publication policy and for allowing a volume on this rather sensitive topic. Our special thanks go to Edwin Gentzler, without whom this volume would not have been possible or probably might never have happened. Edwin was invited to Antwerp for a discussion of his latest book. He was not only welcomed with praise, he was also challenged, all of which has resulted in the works presented here. Only such strong scholarly personalities as Edwin can play down the praise and take the brunt of such criticism in propagating open debate within the discipline.

References

Baker, Mona. 2001. "The Pragmatics of Cross Cultural Contact and Some False Dichotomies in Translation Studies." In *CTIS Occasional Papers*, Vol. 1, edited by Maeve Olohan,7–20. Manchester: Centre for Translation and Intercultural Studies, UMIST.

Barnard, Alan. 2000. *History and Theory in Anthropology*. Cambridge: Cambridge University Press.

Clifford, James &, George Marcus. 1986. *Writing Culture: The Poetics and Politics of Ethnography*. Berkeley: University of California Press.

Gentzler, Edwin. 2008. *Translation and Identity in the Americas: New Directions in Translation Theory*. London/New York: Routledge

Shohat, Ella and Robert Stam. 1994. *Unthinking Eurocentrism: Multiculturalism and the Media*. London/New York: Routledge.

van Doorslaer, Luc. 2010. "The Side Effects of the 'Eurocentrism' Concept." In *Socio-Cultural Approaches to Translation: Indian and European Perspectives*, edited by J. Prabhakara Rao & Jean Peeters, 39–46. New Delhi: Excel India Publishers.

Vinay, Jean-Paul and Jean Darbelnet. 1958. *Stylistique comparée du français et de l'anglais*. Paris: Didier.

Macro- and micro-turns in translation studies

Edwin Gentzler

Definitions of translation studies are changing. While historically focused on the process or product of translation at a national European level, new definitions by scholars such as Mukherjee, Trivedi, Cheung, and Tymoczko are expanding the parameters of translation by exploring how the field is defined in international non-European contexts — in India, China, the Arab world, for example. Other scholars, such as Cronin, Simon, Apter, and Brodzki are looking at subnational locations, including within cities, diasporic communities within cities, and even between generations within individual families in those communities. This paper looks at how translation is defined and studied in such macro- and micro-contexts in the Americas, suggesting that translation is less something that happens between national cultures and more something, especially among immigrants and linguistic minorities, that comprises the very basis upon which those cultures are constructed.

In *In Search of a Theory of Translation* (1980), Gideon Toury called for a temporary suspension of more definitions of translation until more data could be collected. He suggested that scholars define translation as any text "regarded as a translation from the intrinsic point of view of the target system" (1980: 73), despite preconceived criteria or non-conformity with the original. Revolutionary at the time, such a definition opened the field to the study of all sorts of translational phenomena seldom considered under more traditional definitions, including popular culture texts, "substandard" translations, interpretations, adaptations, intersemiotic translations, oral translations, intralingual translations, and even pseudo-translations (no originals). In the last few years, two new trends in translation studies, which I refer to as macro- and micro-turns, terms derived in part from Michael Cronin's *Translation and Identity* (2006) (see below), are again opening up the field to a plethora of translational activity not previously considered, much being observed in non-European settings. By macro-turn I refer to larger international, global, and transnational translation research; by micro-turn I refer to investigations of translation within cities, neighborhoods, and even families.

My research on translational phenomena in the Americas certainly figures in data that often is viewed as exceptional by many European definitions and models. I have no desire to adopt fashionable critical (anti-European) terms for selfish purposes; the empirical reality is that most American nations are made up of a majority of immigrants. The United States, for example, continues to allow into its borders the largest percentage of immigrants in the world. According to a United Nations report, in 2005 the United States accepted 38.4 million immigrants, over three times the nation with the second highest total, which was Russia, with 12.1 million (UN International Migration Report 2006: xvi). Canada is sixth, with 6.1 million immigrants. While in the past most of these immigrants came from European countries, today there are increasing numbers arriving from Latin America and Asia. The percentage of citizens with little or no proficiency in English is on the rise, and rather than assimilate, many are choosing to preserve their language heritage, thereby increasing the need for translation services in many everyday interactions. As cultures comprised of a majority of immigrants, the Americas find that translations are not only more prevalent and more diverse than in Europe, but translation has become a necessary skill in terms of navigating the increasingly multilingual culture. Some European terms for studying translations, such as source/target, same/other, primary/secondary, or original/translation, seem not to apply. In the Americas, the other has often become the same; the original is already in translation. To study these conditions, I do not suggest an "either/or" proposition, positing, for example, an "American" approach to translation as a replacement for European approaches. Indeed, European translation studies has provided a plethora of tools for comparative and historical study. Rather, I offer a "both/and" approach, incorporating both European and non-European insights, thereby growing the field of study. By force or free will, the languages of the Americas are largely European, but always with exceptions.

In the first part of this essay I focus on macro-turns, looking at broader international definitions and movements and how they in turn impact existing, dare I say Eurocentric, definitions. In the second half I focus on what I call micro-turns, including research on smaller, more local geographic spaces, and their impact on the field. Here I give examples from my own research presented in *Translation and Identity in the Americas: New Directions in Translation Theory* (2008).

Part I: Macro-turns in translation studies

In their study of non-European translated texts and traditions, scholars such as Harish Trivedi, Martha Cheung, and Myriam Salama-Carr draw attention to definitions of translation in *international* contexts — India, China, and the Arab world, for example. My investigations of translational phenomena in Canada, Latin America, Brazil, and border cultures, including the Caribbean, can be seen as part of this internationalizing movement. In the macro-region I call the Americas, I suggest that translation is less something that happens *between* cultures and more something that is *constitutive* of those very cultures. I also suggest that translation, more than any other genre, has helped determine cultural identity in many parts of the Americas.

As translation studies grows as a discipline, from its early days in the mid-seventies in the Low Countries to its development as a worldwide discipline today, definitions of the field are changing. Many European definitions of translation related to transferring a text from one language to the other are being expanded to include aspects and connotations present in translated texts and communications in other parts of the world. Definitions of language are changing, challenged by proliferating semiotic codes and sign systems, informed by new technologies for the construction of texts, and complicated by factors associated with dialects and emerging languages. Definitions of what constitutes a text are also changing, as more oral and performative texts are included in studies. Lines between translation, adaptation, abridgement, paraphrase, and summaries are blurring. The question of what constitutes a translation is under radical review. While some scholars are threatened by such an expanding terrain, many others in the field find it quite invigorating. I first look at European definitions of translation and then at more international definitions.

European definitions of translation

In terms of European definitions of 'translation,' there are related but diverging concepts, and so Toury's flexible definition has served the field well. As is well known, the English definition of the word derives from Latin *translatus*, with *trans-* referring to 'across' or 'over' and *latus* referring to 'borne' or 'carried,' resulting in "carried across." The Spanish, French, and Italian definitions of the term derive from a different root, the Latin *traducere* (rather than *translatus*) and thus *traducción/traduction/traduzione* implies 'to alter, change over, transport,' from Latin *traducere* ('change over, convert'), from *trans* plus *ducere* ('to lead') (see words such as 'duke'). Once we move beyond the Latin-derived languages, the process of semantic wandering increases. In German, *Übersetzung* combines *über-* ('over') with *setzen* ('to set' or 'place'), resulting in 'setting over' with its earliest usages meaning to place someone or something in another setting. In Dutch, *vertalen* has a slightly different etymology: *Ver-* refers to the action of doing or performing, moving or changing the manner, but *ver-* also has a negative connotation, as in *werpen* ('throw')/*verwerpen* ('reject'); or *oordelen* ('judge')/*veroordelen* ('condemn'). The stem *talen* refers to language, communication, speech, spoken communication, tongue, and voice communication (probably related to the English word 'talk'), resulting in changing the language/speech. In Russian, the word for translation is *перевод* (perevód), which refers to transfer, remittance, switching, shunting, or conversation. Similar to the English prefix trans-, *pere* refers to 'across', but *vod*, from the verb *vodit'*, refers to 'lead' or 'drive', thus the Russian word allows a more active role for the translator/interpreter to lead, guide, or direct the communication activity, one which is related to how the term is used in Latin America.

While these definitions vary, no doubt leading to variations of the corpora studied by translation scholars in the respective European cultures, there are semantic similarities: metaphors of movement as in carrying across, placing in another setting, transporting, leading, and guiding predominate, assuming different sides/languages/cultures and the action of moving words/texts/meanings across a divide.

Non-European definitions of translation

One of the directions in which translation studies is currently headed is beyond Latin, Germanic, and Slavic definitions in order to consider connotations of the concept 'translation' in non-European terms. Here data is still being collected. Three sources have been particularly influential. In *Translating Others* (2006), Theo Hermans has collected multiple essays by scholars who have taken the international turn, including Martha Cheung (Chinese), Harish Trivedi (India), and Myriam Salama-Carr (Arabic). In *Asian Translation Traditions* (2005), Eva Hung and Judy Wakabayashi assembled the work of authors who have taken the "Asian turn" in translation studies, including Wakabayashi herself (Japanese, but also Chinese and Vietnamese), Theresa Hyun (Korean), and Keith Taylor (Vietnamese). In *Enlarging Translation, Empowering Translators* (2007), Maria Tymoczko includes a section on "Conceptualizations of Translation Worldwide," which begins with the Irish-British conflict but quickly turns to non-European concepts, including definitions not only from China, India, and the Arabic world, but also from Indonesia, Nigeria, and the Philippines, indicative of a multiplicity of macro-turns. While many of these definitions have histories longer than those of similar terms in Europe, the recent exchange of ideas and scholarship between East and West is enriching the field.

In India, for example, Tymoczko cites two common words for translation — Sanskrit/Indian: *rupantar*, referring to 'change in form', and *anuvad*, referring to 'speaking after' or 'following' (Tymoczko 2007:68) — and suggests that neither implies fidelity to the original. Sujit Mukherjee (1994:80) suggests that the fields of association for these terms include both translation and transcreation, and that alteration and variation are permissible; this definition shares similarities with definitions of translation as transcreation emerging in countries such as Mexico or Brazil. Harish Trivedi (2006: 113) suggests that *anuvad* implies a temporal process (speaking after) rather than a spatial one (carrying across) invoked by the Western term. Another word for translation used in India is *chaya*, referring to 'shadow' or 'counterpart.' Mukherjee suggests that this term recalls a form of following on the heels of the source text as a shadow trails a person, appearing differently depending upon the angle from which the translator interprets. Furthermore, Trivedi suggests that there is a striking *absence* of translation from foreign languages as a textual practice. Much of the translation in India is internal, — oral, or even unspoken — as many of the languages spoken there, such as Sanskrit and Prakrit, are mutually intelligible. Translation as it is understood in the West, he suggests, only arrived in India with the European colonization (Trivedi 2006: 105–6; see Tymoczko 2007: 69).

Probably the most widespread work on international definitions of translation derives from thinking about the Chinese term *fanyi*, which includes the reference to 'turning over.' *Fan* refers to 'turning', 'flipping', or 'somersaulting'; *yi* refers to 'interpreting' but can also invoke 'exchange.' In "'To Translate' Means 'To Exchange'? A New Interpretation of the Earliest Chinese Attempts to Define Translation ('Fanyi')" (2006), Martha Cheung argues that for many centuries the two words *fan* and *yi* were both used independently of each other to refer to 'translation'; only in the twelfth century were they combined. Cheung suggests that the concept *fanyi* involves two sides of the same coin/leaf/embroidery and so posits translation as both front and back, yet facing in opposite directions (Cheung 2006: 177; see Tymoczko 2007: 72). When considering translation in the Americas, first as colonies then later as independent nations, this concept of neither one nor the other (source or target) but simultaneously both, transnationally interdependent, is of increasing relevance.

Another scholar working to uncover forms of translation not normally investigated as such is Judy Wakabayashi, who in "Translation in the East Asian Cultural Sphere: Shared Roots, Divergent Paths?" (2005) talks about hidden translation in the Chinese cultural sphere. In China, as is well known, many languages are spoken, but they all share the same written tradition. Wakabayashi suggests that the different language groups in China are often performing acts of a silent "mental translation." (2005: 24–25). The written Chinese characters lend themselves to the generation of any number of translations into other languages and dialects. The use of Mandarin as a kind of *lingua franca* has served the Chinese nation-state well, ensuring cross-cultural communication within the country with no need for written translations, but there are costs. Certainly images of classical concepts, earlier Chinese civilizations, imperial Chinese meanings, are carried forth to the present, via visual, textual, and audio connotations present in an ideographic writing system, which can conceivably suppress alternative concepts and more local interpretations. Wakabayashi suggests that the Chinese officials use this system of non-written translation as a means of extending their imperialistic and hegemonic worldview. Harsh words, but ones that tangentially apply to the "mental translation" imposed on the Americas, particularly in so-called "monolingual" countries such as the United States, where immigrants are forced to translate themselves into the dominant English-only culture.

To cite one more example, the most common Arabic word for translation is *tarjama*, which originally referred to 'biography' (Naous 2007). Tymoczko speculates that the term derives from the early Christian translators of the Bible and authors of lives of the saints during the third to fifth century. She further suggests that the term allows for a certain amount of agency by the translator insofar as the translator is the one who narrates the story and thus frames the reception, which supports her view of the translator's political role (Tymoczko 2007:71). A second meaning of *tarjama* involves 'definition,' which connects well to the great period of Arabic translation of Greek texts, especially scientific and mathematical ones. In "Translation into Arabic in the 'Classical Age'" (2006), about the Baghdad School of translation during the ninth and tenth centuries, Myriam Salama-Carr points out that translators were viewed as scholars in their own right, at the same level as the authors. As I argue in *Translation and Identity in the Americas* (2008), in all the new nations of the Americas, the connection of translation to the construction of one's own identity is deep and ongoing, and translation plays a primary rather than secondary role in the construction of the identity of individuals in those cultures. Suzanne Jill Levine, for example, writes, "Translation is a mode of writing that might enable one to find one's own language through another's." (1991:2; qtd. by Gentzler 2008:34). I suggest that the pursuit of the etymological connections of *tarjama* to biography in Arabic may greatly inform the field of translation studies as it expands in the future, especially among those scholars conducting research on the lives of translators.

New directions in the Americas

Such international definitions have helped me rethink the translation landscape as I examined various translation approaches prevalent in Canada, Latin America, Brazil, and the Caribbean. I focus here on Canada and Brazil, countries with arguably the most advanced translation studies research paradigms in the hemisphere. In Canada, the *joual* (a deformation of *cheval*, or 'horse') movement during the 1970s and 80s found itself thoroughly intertwined with the independence movement in Quebec. Since *joual* was an unofficial language, a working-class dialect of

French with heavy American interference spoken in the streets of Montreal and Quebec, there were no written texts but only oral manifestations. Then a group of translators and playwrights started writing and translating into *joual* pieces for the stage. Theater translators in Quebec, including such writers/translators as Robert Lalonde, Michel Garneau, Jean Claude Germain, and Michel Trembley, began translating not into "standard" French but into hybridized forms of the French language. The most common form used by the playwrights was *joual*, but other forms used by translators as target languages included archaic French, Gaspéan French, and other regional dialects. Studying the *joual* movement serves as a mini-laboratory for thinking about how linguistic minorities can use translation to resist hegemonic language policies and to create openings for new modes of expression.

In *A Sociocritique of Translation: Theatre and Alterity in Quebec 1968–1988* (1996), Annie Brisset described this multilingual, polyvalent target culture as a "translational" culture insofar as the people of Quebec were aware of the markers and cultural codes that invade their culture via translations, copies, imitations, and images of both French and Anglo-American culture. This flood of images, often perpetuated by official translation policies of the nation-state, served, Brisset asserted, merely to continue the colonization of the Quebecois, precluding their independent development. In an ironic reversal, Brisset argued that in theater translation in Quebec during this period, translators were less concerned with bringing the original across a linguistic border and more focused on a *rejection* of the original, which in turn opened up a space for the invention of a national language derived from Québécois French, *joual*, immigrant French, and other working class and rural dialects. She also claimed that Michel Garneau's translation of *Macbeth* became one of the most important literary texts of the time, turning Shakespeare into the "Québécois national poet" (1996: 109). Most scholars agree that the *joual* movement has receded, and indeed theaters that were producing 80–90% of their plays in Québécois French have now returned to staging their plays in standard French. However, one should not underestimate the power of translation to effect cultural change; in the 1990s, the Bloc Québécois, fueled in large part by linguistic and translation policies, became the second largest party in Quebec, with the 1995 referendum on independence failing by just percentage points (50.6 % to 49.4%). The success of this regional/national movement must be of interest both to scholars studying translation in postcolonial and emerging nations and to scholars studying linguistic minorities and translation within larger nation-states. Furthermore, some scholars, such as Sherry Simon, suggest that the translation movement has expanded to include post-translation and increasingly multilingual cultural interventions in art, architecture, design, and even creative writing (see below). In theater translation alone, plays such as *Le Making of de Macbeth* (1996), which is a play about a director considering whether or not to stage Garneau's

Macbeth, ultimately deciding *against* its production, continue to employ hybrid bilingual language forms begun during the *joual* movement and underscore the need to produce plays that reflect the multiplicity of languages, dialects, and immigrant experiences characteristic of contemporary Québécois culture.

Similar to the Canadian theater translators who use translation as a mode of cultural creation, a group of translators and artists in Brazil are using a form of translation called "cannibalism" to challenge European models and to construct their own alternative. Known as the *movimento antropofágico* (cannibalist movement), founded by Oswald de Andrade in 1928 with the "Manifesto Antropófago," the group was one of several related movements in Latin America during the 1920s and 1930s. It more or less disappeared from view in the West until resurrected by successive groups of translators, first by the brothers Haroldo and Augusto de Campos in the mid 1960s, then by filmmakers such as Joaquim Pedro de Andrade, Glauber Rocha, Nelson Pereira dos Santos in the late 1960s early 1970s, then by musicians such as Caetano Veloso in the 1970s and 80s, and most recently by critics and theorists such as Else Vieira, Sergio Bellei, Roberto Schwarz, and Nelson Arscher in the 1980s and 1990s.

In "Tupy or not Tupy: Cannibalism and Nationalism in Contemporary Brazilian Literature" (1987), Brazilian literary and film critic Randall Johnson suggests that cannibalism was an aggressive conceit aimed at shocking the Eurocentric bourgeoisie. Cannibalism combined native elements and a more historical and complex socio-religious connection to the indigenous peoples who practiced such acts. It was used as a vehicle to explore the past and the process of evolution of Brazilian national culture. Tracing the blood of the Native American allowed access to multiple ethnic, moral, geographic, and political elements that have always been part of the Brazilian identity. The cannibal metaphor was understood in Brazil as a distinct form of resistance to European culture and a form of nourishing one's own. In Brazil, it symbolized an end to the imitation, an end to translation in a traditional sense, and the beginning of the creation of an alternative to European culture. Copying and importing art, politics, social forms was at an end; devouring it, adapting it, rejecting the negative, embracing the positive was just beginning. Translation, which in the past had served primarily as an uncritical medium to import European culture, became one of the critical tools used to consume and digest European ideas and then to reelaborate them in terms of native traditions and conditions. In sum, it marks the end of mental colonization and the beginning of an independent identity formation in Brazil.

Some translation scholars suggest that the cannibalist movement was short-lived, elitist, and practiced by just a few famous translators. Unlike the *joual* movement, which has died down, or better said, has transformed itself into a more multicultural movement, the cannibalist movement is very much alive: artists are importing forms and expressions not just from Europe but from Asia and Africa as well; musicians are importing and adapting music from North America and Africa; and favela artists are "cannibalizing" whatever they can get their hands on. As the poet Diana Menasché made clear in a reading at the University of Massachusetts in March 2011, even patients in mental health clinics in Brazil are cannibalizing psychoanalytical discourse and making it their own. Indeed, in cultures primarily made up of immigrants, it should come as no surprise that a translation strategy of importation, adaptation, and cannibalization is central to cultural formation. Indeed, the question is not whether cannibalization is still alive but the extent to which it applies to all translation, in Europe and elsewhere.

The thread that ties together the macro-turns, the ongoing investigations by non-European scholars in translation studies, is the idea that translation is less a mechanical activity done by some sort of scribe in a neutral fashion between two separate and distinct cultures and languages than it is a *defining* activity done by human beings with vested interests, and that this activity *constitutes* the very culture in which they live. Culture in the Americas has always been a translational culture. While the ideas of the Americas are expressed in European languages, those languages are not totally owned by anyone. Indeed, in André Lefevere's words, the European languages are being rewritten in the American vein. By rewriting, reinterpreting, and translating, by incorporating bits and pieces from a variety of cultures — the colonizing European powers, other European cultures, other immigrant groups, and indigenous ideas, myths, and natural elements — the Americas are still very much under construction. And this construction is not top-down, linearly lateral, or rational, but bottom-up, multidirectional, and often accidental. Translation, I suggest, plays an important part, if not the most important part, in that construction.

Translation, therefore, when viewed from the larger, international, or macro-perspective, is often used as both a mode of understanding — coming to terms with indigenous roots, international and cross-cultural ties, and growing interrelations with other translational cultures — and as a creative/recreative act — allowing new forms, relations, and modes of expression to surface. Translation in this wider sense moves in strange, labyrinthine patterns and is yet to be codified by scholars. Because of its often cannibalistic and constitutive nature, as seen in the examples presented, I suggest that scholars need to exercise caution in applying static, reductive definitions that limit insight and growth.

Part II: Micro-turns in translation studies

In *Translation and Identity* (2006), Irish translation theorist Michael Cronin looks at translation in the city rather than the nation or nation-state. The cities that interest Cronin are less the long-established cultural capitals, such as Athens, Alexandria, Rome, Paris, and London, and more the new emerging world cities, such as São Paulo, Mexico City, Montreal, Hong Kong, and Shanghai. The city represents for Cronin a structure comprised of clusters of individuals, a locus that is particularly conducive to translation. For those individuals living in different communities within the city, translation is seen as the most important vehicle for accessing different information, allowing for cultural and linguistic integrity while at the same time facilitating a wider circulation of concepts, ideas, and cognitive styles (Cronin 2006: 139). He coins the term "micro-cosmopolitan," from which derives the title of this section, to refer to this different form of thinking about geographic units within cosmopolitan centers. Cronin suggests scholars turn to a form of thinking about cities that is derived from a "bottom-up" process of localization rather than a top-down process of globalization. There are no outsiders or insiders in such a model; rather the difference is found within by paying attention to the complexity of the make-up of any given city. Perhaps scholars need to think less in terms of translation from language to language, or nation to nation, and more in terms of movement and migrations between and within cities.

In *Translating Montreal: Episodes in the Life of a Divided City* (2006), Canadian translation theorist Sherry Simon also turns to the unit of the city to investigate translational phenomena. She questions the limits of earlier definitions of translation and focuses instead on the conditions conducive to translation, such as the multicultural life in the city of Montreal and the hybrid forms of communication there, many of which take place before and after the actual act of translation. Indeed, Montreal provides a perfect laboratory for her study. Already a bilingual city, officially French (52%) and English (18%), the French in Montreal is already diverse, including standard, working-class, Québécois, *joual*, North African, Caribbean, and Anglo-American versions. The immigrant languages (27%) are also many, including Irish, Italian, Portuguese, Greek, Arabic, Hebrew and Yiddish, Chinese, Haitian, and most recently, Latin American Spanish, not to mention the First Nation languages (3%), including Cree, Inuktitut, and Ojibway. Simon discusses the people and places in the various ethnic neighborhoods of Montreal, including Chinatown, Latin Quarter, and Little Italy, as well as the multicultural areas such as Mile End, and shows how the artists, poets, playwrights, and architects of Montreal use translation on a regular basis, consciously or subconsciously, in their creative work. At a certain point, translation disappears into the "original" creative texts as they blend into new texts that invigorate the complex multicultural urban space, to the point that translation and original writing are indistinguishable. Indicative of the new directions translation theory is taking in the Americas, she offers a new definition: "I give translation an expanded definition in this book: writing that is inspired by the encounter with other tongues, including the effects of creative interference" (Simon 2006: 17).

In *The Translation Zone: A New Comparative Literature* (2006), U. S. translation theorist Emily Apter uses the word "zone" to refer to a space that is not defined by language, politics, nation, race, or class, but by smaller sites of translational activity. She worries that those who decide language and domestic cultural policy also decide translation policy, which in turn affects textual heritage, preservation, and dissemination. She wants to alter the units studied by translation studies scholars and to recognize new sites of language contact as battlegrounds on which the survival of languages and the ethnic and cultural memories embedded within them depend. Apter looks at micro-translation sites — diasporic language communities, border cultures, media spheres, and departments in universities. She asks what gets translated and, especially, what does not, focusing on caesura, omissions, transmission failures, and that which is deemed untranslatable. She suggests that the translation zone is a *political* zone, a medium for social and political formation and reformation. She looks at governmental involvement in domestic and foreign policies, such as how translations are used in espionage and military engagements. Indeed, one of the strengths of the book is the way translation and military policies are intertwined, suggesting the political urgency for more and better translation in the precarious post-9/11 world.

Finally, in *Can these Bones Live: Translation, Survival, and Cultural Memory* (2007), U.S. translation theorist Bella Brodzki talks about even smaller units for the study of translation, in this case often within a family, such as inter-generational translation passed along from mother to daughter, or grandparent to grandchild. Invoking Benjamin's concept of the afterlife of translation, Brodzki presents this kind of translation as often elusive insofar as it is oral rather than written and may be repressed because of its often traumatic nature. Her case studies include translation for refugees, exiles, and immigrants, who oftentimes have moved or been moved under the most trying of circumstances: Jews fleeing Nazi Germany or Africans fleeing dictators. She also refers repeatedly to literary texts, such as Maxine Hong Kingston's *Woman Warrior* (1975), which concerns a "translation" of her mother's confusing "talk story," involving translation on a number of levels, although it is seldom called a translation. For Brodzki, translation is an act of recovery, a life-sustaining act, and a life-empowering moment shared between two generations and across complex cultural, historical, and linguistic divides. Translation becomes a form of cultural memory and survival.

Multilingual United States

In many studies of translation and globalization, the United States is analyzed along the lines of its economic and sociological homogenizing tendencies, more often than not viewed as the new imperial international power, subjugating ethnic and linguistic minorities by using policies initiated during the period of European colonization. While this is unquestionably true, and one cannot deny the English-only trend in the electronic age of communication, my investigations focus less on the English-only trends in the United States, and more on the non-English and translational developments. Although the United States is considered a "mono-lingual" country, the fact is that over 150 languages are spoken in the country, and one out of five "Americans" is born into a non-English-speaking or limited-English-speaking families. Most of the translation that takes place in the country takes place in the inner cities, in regional communities, ethnic neighborhoods, and within families, yet these translations, mostly oral, are seldom studied by scholars. Here is a list of the top ten languages spoken in the USA and the number of speakers (United States Census Bureau 2006):

US Census 2006: Language spoken at home	Number
Total population 5 years old and over	279,012,712
1. English	224,154,288
2. Spanish or Spanish Creole	34,044,945
3. Chinese	2,492,871
4. Tagalog	1,415,599
5. Vietnamese	1,207,721
6. German	1,135,999
7. Russian	823,210
8. Polish	640,265
9. Hindi	504,607
10. Urdu	324,578
Other Indic languages	612,890

These numbers are of course not entirely accurate, as non-English languages speakers are historically underrepresented in census counts, and the figures are dated. Many estimate that the Spanish-speaking population is now (as of early 2010) over 45 million. Chinese figures are probably too low by over 500,000. Furthermore, if one looks at more local populations at the state and city level, the number of non-English speakers is even more startling (United States Census Bureau 2006):

City	Population	English	Non-English	Percent
New York	7,637,820	3,981,767	3,656,053	47.9
Patterson, NJ	136,498	57,363	79,135	58.0
Boston	539,223	352,255	186,969	34.7
Miami	333,755	79,383	254,372	76.2
San Francisco	703,169	376,801	326,368	46.4
Santa Ana, Ca	314,820	54,142	260,678	82.8
Dallas	1,082,672	612,828	469,844	43.4
Brownsville, Tx	154,850	17,837	137,013	88.5

Again, these figures are dated; some estimate that in Boston the number of non-English speakers has now surpassed that of English speakers. Still, the numbers are revealing: today in many cities in the United States, non-English-speakers outnumber English speakers.

If one looks at even more micro-geographic units, such as the inner city, or at certain neighborhoods within cities, such as the various Chinatowns and Little Italies, English further recedes in dominance, and the dramatic need for translation in almost every public exchange increases. One of the reasons there is so much poverty and ghettoization in the culture of the United States is that the parts that do not fit — invariably those of a different color, ethnicity, culture, and language — are often cast aside. Examples include Amerindians relegated to reservations, Chinese immigrants centralized in Chinatowns, blacks impoverished in urban ghettos, Latinos centralized in barrios, and many ethnic minorities and non-English speakers, mostly men, incarcerated in a disproportionate fashion. With no translation policy, no policy of mediation, negotiation, or communication, there is no other place to put them. The expulsion, however, is never complete; if one looks closely enough, the multilingual nature of the American citizenry is everywhere to be seen. In my work, I suggest that the two are not mutually exclusive: monolingualism always includes multilingualism, although it hides the very multilingual foundation upon which it rests.

In the second chapter of *Translation and Identity in the Americas*, I cite a definition of translation by Derrida that appears in *Monolingualism of the Other* (1998). For Derrida, translation is a fundamental cultural necessity, even in a monolingual country, always present yet hidden or *sous rature*. Derrida writes:

> — *We only ever speak one language …*
>   (*yes, but*)
> — *We never speak only one language …*
> is not only the very law of what is called translation. It would also be the law itself as translation. A law which is a little mad, I grant you that. (1998:10, italics in original)

Derrida's thinking about monolingualism of the Other is dependent upon this on-going but hidden (possible-impossible; allowed-forbidden) process of translation. The kind of translation Derrida discusses here is not the conventional, interlingual, type of translation, but another, partially "mad," quasi-schizophrenic, psycho-so-cial kind of translation that underlies any given monolingual cultural condition. As translation studies turns to micro-investigations, I suggest that the field remain open to consider such psychological and social factors. In the case of the United States, all the multiple hyphenated identities, including African-American, Asian-American, French-American, or more local hybridizations, such as Chicano, Newyorican, or Rastacadian, indicate the schizophrenic nature of the "united" culture of the United States and suggest the difficulty of ever arriving at a unified monolingual "American" identity. This schizophrenic psychological space might be most visible in its reverse construction; those language and ethnic minorities living within the English-only dominant culture know only too well what it means to be identified as carrying out any particular "Un-American" activity. There is a kind of madness in this out-of-sight translation, one that implies a continual pro-cess of simultaneous linguistic oppression and resistance to that very oppression.

The occasion at which Derrida presented his ideas about *Monolingualism of the Other* was a conference in New Orleans attended by Francophone scholars from the Francophone United States, the Caribbean, Canada, Belgium, Switzerland, Africa, and France. Derrida attended largely because of his friend Abdelkebir Khatibi, author of *Amour bilingue* (1990), a book which has engendered much discussion on bilingualism and translation. As both Derrida and Khatibi are Franco-Maghrebian, much of the discussion centered on their growing up in a monolingual culture (French) in which their Arabic, Berber, and in the case of Derrida, Jewish, cultures and languages were suppressed. At the time, access to any non-French language, such as academic or colloquial Arabic or Berber, was pro-hibited. In Algeria, the only option for studying Arabic was in the schools, where it could only be studied as a *foreign* language. Derrida talks candidly about the psycho- and social-pathological trauma endured by people in such a situation, the *unheimlich* feeling of always being an outsider in your home country, as well as the discrimination, beatings, murders, and even state-supported assassinations that took place because of the language gap. While Khatibi does write in his "mother tongue," which is French, it is a French in which other language codes — Arabic, Berber, Spanish, Italian, with traces of Greek and Persian — are embedded, a kind of secret code that only multilinguals can translate and understand.

Abdelkebir Khatibi is well known in translation theory circles; his work is discussed in Samia Mehrez's seminal essay "Translation and the Postcolonial Experience: The Francophone North African Text" (1992). Mehrez discusses the influence that ethnic minorities in North Africa have on translation theory, and her work provides insights for the study of translation in the Americas. The languages of North Africa forge new hybrid language groups that defy translation, notions of equivalence, and ideas of loss and gain via translation. As similar ethnic minorities move to the urban areas of the United States, I suggest that translation theory in these areas will be equally challenged and redefined. Mehrez shows how Khatibi does not merely reflect on the difficulty of translating the language of the Other but also uses the Other to invade the space of the Same to create a *secret translation discourse* from within. Mehrez writes, "Not that I am referring to a process whereby the language of the Other becomes unrecognizable, or deformed. Rather, the process is one where the language of the Other comes to encode messages which are not readily decoded by the monolingual reader" (1992:122). I suggest that at such a micro-level, translation scholars need to be alert to this hidden, encoded form of translation used by minority groups. The trick used by many minority translators and creative writers is to *avoid* assimilation into the dominant language and culture of the majority, using translation as a tool to evade, expand, enrich, and diversify existing codes of signification. For Khatibi, as for similar language minorities, translation is an always ongoing process that cannot be separated from writing in any individual language. He writes, "The 'maternal' language is always at work in the foreign language. Between them occurs a constant process of translation, an abysmal dialogue, very difficult to bring to the light of day" (Khatibi 1981:8; quoted by Mehrez 1992:134; trans. by Mehrez).

In *Monolingualism of the Other*, Derrida identifies with Khatibi's particular situation in Northern Africa, but his discussion of the institutional insistence of monolingualism and its imposition on non- or limited-speaking citizens applies to other cultures as well. It may seem a stretch to apply postcolonial theories of translation in North Africa to the situation in the United States, one of the world's imperial powers, but the connection can be useful. For example, the conference took place in New Orleans, where French, the dominant language of the original settlers and *de facto* official language of colonial Louisiana, was long the majority language of Louisianans. Indeed, in the nineteenth century, the cultural capital was New Orleans, and French poetry, theater, music, dance, food, and architecture thrived. A wealth of French histories, fiction, poetry, and drama emerged, most written in Creole French, including Henry Rémy's histories, Louis-Armand Garreau's novels, and Julien Poydras's poetry. With the state constitution of 1913, however, French ceased to be recognized and was officially eliminated from the public sphere as well as indirectly discriminated against in private society; Cajuns were verbally harassed, referred to as backward, retarded, hedonists, swamp dwellers, and web-footed. French-speaking men and boys were beaten, women and girls were raped, and, as in Algeria, many incarcerated and murdered. Serious efforts at monolingualism and assimilation have continued through English-only politics to the present; even today, despite efforts of Cajun activists and the creation of the state agency The Council for the Development of French in Louisiana (CODOFIL), the status of French remains quite low. No translation legislation exists, although Cajuns are the second largest minority, after African-Americans, in the region; French can only be studied in school as a foreign language, despite the fact that 261,678 Louisianans speak French in their homes and over one million claim francophone origin (Landry and Allard, 1996: 449).

In light of the conference that was held in December 2009 in Antwerp in which these discussions of "Eurocentrism and the Americas" began, and the number of Belgian scholars participating in this collection, I turn to the case of the Low Countries' colony of New Netherlands, where most of the narrative histories and archival materials were written in Dutch. Unlike the French example above, which involves ongoing language oppression, the Dutch example serves to illustrate historical linguistic and cultural loss, which I suggest has been detrimental to the construction of American identity in the present. The micro-area in question is the city of New Amsterdam, which at the time covered only the southern tip of the Island of Manhattan. Surprisingly, the area has grown to be the current financial capital of the country, and some might argue, the world. At the time, Holland was among the most liberal nations in Europe — the Puritans, for example, escaped from England to Leiden, Holland, and lived there for twelve years before moving to America. While New Amsterdam was founded by the Low Countries as a trading post under the auspices of the Dutch West Indies Company, according to Russell Shorto, author of The Island at the Center of the World (2005), over *half* of its residents were from other parts of the world, including Swedes, Norwegians, Germans, Italians, Jews, Africans (slaves and free), English, including those excommunicated from the Puritan British colony to the North, and Native Americans, including Montauks, Mahicans, Housatonics, and Mohawks (Shorto 2005: 2). New Amsterdam became one of the first multiethnic, multicultural, and multilingual cities in the world. People from all over Europe came to ports such as Antwerp to emigrate to the colony, including the Dutch, Spaniards, Germans, Slavs, Italians, Blacks, Jews, Protestants, as well as many persecuted groups. Shorto suggests that its influence on the cultural evolution and identity of United States citizens is just as important, if not more so, than the cultural heritage of the British in New England or Virginia. He writes, "If what made America great was its ingenious openness to different cultures, then the small triangle of land at the southern tip of Manhattan Island is the New World birthplace of that idea" (2005: 3).

Historians have told us little of that period; the most an average United States citizen knows is that the Dutch bought the island in 1626 from the Indians for 60 guilders (about 24 dollars). Yet a massive storehouse of records exists — by some estimates over 12,000 pages stored in archives in New York, Albany, and

Amsterdam, many of which remain untranslated. Yet due to the efforts of unsung translators, such as Charles Gehring, Director of the New Netherlands Project, who has devoted thirty years of his life to translating such material (Gehring 1981, 1995, 2000), this historical record is coming to light. Documents include political agreements, laws, letters, journals, court cases, ship records, military records, trade records, and any number of miscellaneous documents about drinking, fights, thefts, marital infidelities, and land disputes. I suggest that these translated texts illustrate national traits that are, perhaps, more indicative of the United States' identity than many of the English so-called foundational texts. Whereas in the English colony to the north, English predominated, in New Amsterdam, over eighteen languages could be heard. Whereas in the Puritan colony, only one religion was tolerated, in the Dutch colony, religious differences were tolerated, with Protestants, Anglicans, Catholics, English Pilgrims, Jews, Lutherans, Calvinists, refugees from various lands to the south, and indigenous peoples practicing various native religions. In 1579, the Dutch were one of the first countries in Europe to write into their constitution that "no one shall be persecuted or investigated because of their religion" (Shorto, 2005:96), and thus Amsterdam became one of the most tolerant and diverse cities in Europe, much of which was "translated" to New Amsterdam in the 1600s. In the United States today, the prevailing sense of freedom of religion, openness to immigrants, especially those persecuted in their home countries, and a commitment to equality and diversity may derive more from New York's non-English cultural and linguistic heritage than from its later English period. I suggest the seeds for a multicultural society originated in the multicultural Dutch colony. Shorto writes:

> The Dutch — traders and sailors whose focus was always *out there*: on other lands, other peoples, and their products — had always to put up with differences. Just as foreign goods moved in and out of their ports, foreign ideas, and, for that matter, foreign people did as well. To talk about "celebrating diversity" is to be wildly anachronistic, but in the Europe of the time, the Dutch stood out for their relative acceptance of foreignness, or religious differences, or odd sorts. (2005:26)

While Shorto perhaps romanticizes the Dutch importance in the history of New York and the Americas, missing some of the over-emphasis on trade, capitalism (including trading in slaves), and free markets, his argument that many of the multilingual and multicultural roots of the country can be seen in the Dutch language writings is persuasive. This non-English micro-culture with its own narratives of movement and migration is every bit as exciting and daring as the Anglo-American micro-cultures to the north and south, as documented by the "canonical" writings of the British colonizers such as William Bradford in Massachusetts or John Smith in Virginia.

Conclusion

Translation studies in the United States is in its infant stages: of the thousands of universities in the US, fewer than 20 have post-graduate programs in translation, and only three have PhD programs. Scholars have of necessity adopted and adapted European models, and some argue that even the post-colonial scholarship in translation as practiced in the United States tends toward being yet another Western theory. As far as I know, no one is working on the history of translation *within* the United States, thus the history of translation into English is yet to be written, not to mention the multidirectional French, Spanish, German, African, Greek, Italian, Irish, Mexican, Central American, Chinese, Filipino, Vietnamese, and Indian histories, which remain unexplored, buried in archives in non-English languages, or, more often than not, existing only in unrecorded oral histories, waiting for discovery and translation. This hidden translation history, or better said, micro-histories, of which I speak, is best seen and heard in the 149 non-English languages of the United States. Unfortunately, it can no longer be seen and heard in the over 50 indigenous and slave languages that have disappeared at a great linguistic and cultural cost.

As the Americas are comprised of nations of immigrants, the languages and cultures of *all* the immigrants groups that form the multilingual fabric of the countries are in need of transcription, translation, and further study. Herein the scholars undertaking macro-investigations, with their study of international and transnational connections, might work together with the scholars conducting micro-investigations, with their study of indigenous roots and local immigrant communities, thereby bringing into view translational interrelations in both traditional and non-traditional guises. I lobby for new, open, and less prescriptive definitions and models in order to gather more information and to begin the process of rethinking our understanding of the multiple phenomena of translation. Here a combination of approaches — European and non-European together — might best serve the field, transnationally informing each other and intranationally bringing to light hitherto unexamined phenomena. By studying the macro- and micro-twists and turns of translation, scholars may find that the multilingual, multicultural, and multidirectional aspects of translation are more indicative of the nature of translation than some earlier, more nation-based definitions, delimiting the field of study during its formative stages.

References

Andrade, Oswald de. 1928. "Manifesto Antropófago," trans. Leslie Barry. *Latin American Literary Review* 14.27 (Jan.-June):184–87.

Apter, Emily. 2006. *The Translation Zone: A New Comparative Literature.* Princeton: Princeton University Press.

Brisset, Annie. 1996. *A Sociocritique of Translation: Theatre and Alterity in Quebec 1968-1988,* trans. Rosalind Gill and Roger Gannon. Toronto: University of Toronto Press.

Brodzki, Bella. 2007. *Can these Bones Live: Translation, Survival, and Cultural Memory.* Stanford: Stanford University Press.

Cheung, Martha. 2005. "'To Translate' Means 'To Exchange'? A New Interpretation of the Earliest Chinese Attempts to Define Translation ('Fanyi')." *Target* 17.1: 27–48.

Cheung, Martha, ed. 2006. *An Anthology of Chinese Discourse on Translation,* vol. 1. Manchester: St. Jerome.

Cronin, Michael. 2006. *Translation and Identity.* London: Routledge.

Derrida, Jacques. 1998. *Monolingualism of the Other; or The Prosthesis of Origin,* trans. Patrick Mensah. Stanford: Stanford University Press.

Gentzler, Edwin. 2008. *Translation and Identity in the Americas: New Directions in Translation Theory.* London: Routledge.

Gehring, Charles T., trans. 1981. *Delaware Papers: Dutch Period 1648-64.* New York Historical Manuscripts Series. Baltimore: Genealogical Publishing Co.

Gehring, Charles T., trans. and ed. 1995. *Council Minutes 1655-56.* New Netherlands Document Series. Syracuse: Syracuse University Press.

Gehring, Charles T., trans. and ed. 2000. *Correspondence 1647-63.* New Netherlands Document Series. Syracuse: Syracuse University Press.

Hermans, Theo, ed. 2006. *Translating Others.* 2 vols. Manchester: St. Jerome.

Hung, Eva, and Judy Wakabayashi, eds. 2005. *Asian Translation Traditions.* Manchester: St. Jerome.

Hyun, Theresa M. 2005. "The Lover's Silence, The People's Voice: Translating Nationalist Poetics in the Colonial Period in Korea." In *Asian Translation Traditions,* edited by Eva Hung and Judy Wakabayashi, 67–107. Manchester: St. Jerome.

Johnson, Randal. 1987. "Tupy or not Tupy: Cannibalism and Nationalism in Contemporary Brazilian Literature." In *Modern Latin American Fiction,* edited by John King, 41–59. London: Faber and Faber.

Khatibi, Abdelkebir. 1990. *Amour bilingue,* trans. Richard Howard. Minneapolis: University of Minnesota Press.

Landry, Rodriguez, and Réal Allard. 1996. "French in South Louisiana: Towards Language Loss." *Journal of Multilingual and Multicultural Development* 17.6: 442–68.

Mehrez, Samia. 1992. "Translation and the Postcolonial Experience: The Francophone North African Text." In *Rethinking Translation: Discourse, Subjectivity, Ideology,* edited by Lawrence Venuti, 120–38. London: Routledge..

Menasché, Diana. 2011. "Concrete Poetry — Poesia concreta." Talk and reading. Amherst: University of Massachusetts.

Mukherjee, Sujit. 1994. *Translation as Discovery and Other Essays on Indian Literature in English Translation.* 2nd ed. London: Sangam Books.

Naous, Mazen. 2007. "Opaque Words: Arabic Importations at the Limits of Translation." Unpublished dissertation. University of Massachusetts Amherst.

Oxford English Dictionary Online: http://www.oed.com/, accessed 15 November 2009.

Salama-Carr, Myriam. 2006. "Translation into Arabic in the 'Classical Age': When the Pandora's Box of Transmission Opens ..." In *Translating Others*, Vol. 1, edited by Theo Hermans, 120–31. Manchester: St. Jerome.

Shorto, Russell. 2005. *The Island at the Center of the World*. New York: Vintage.

Simon, Sherry. 1996. *Gender in Translation: Cultural Identity and the Politics of Transmission*. London: Routledge.

Simon, Sherry. 2006. *Translating Montreal: Episodes in the Life of a Divided City*. Montreal: McGill-Queen's University Press.

Taylor, Keith Weller. 2005. "Sino-Vietnamese Translation from Classical to Vernacular." In *Asian Translation Traditions*, edited by Eva Hung and Judy Wakabayashi, 169–94. Manchester: St. Jerome.

Toury, Gideon. 1980. *In Search of a Theory of Translation*. Tel Aviv: The Porter Institute for Poetics and Semiotics.

Trivedi, Harish. 2006. "In Our Own Time, On Our Own Terms: 'Translation' in India." In *Translating Others*, Vol. 1, edited by Theo Hermans, 102–19. Manchester: St. Jerome,.

Tymoczko, Maria. 2007. *Enlarging Translation, Empowering Translators*. Manchester: St. Jerome, 2007.

United Nations, Department of Economic and Social Affairs, Population Division, *International Migration Report 2006: A Global Assessment*. New York: United Nations, 2009. http://www.un.org/esa/population/publications/2006_MigrationRep/exec_sum.pdf, accessed 13 May 2011.

United States Census Bureau. 2000. Languages Spoken at Home. http://www.census.gov/compendia/statab/cats/population/ancestry_language_spoken_at_home.html, accessed 21 November 2009.

United States Census Bureau. 2006. American Community Survey. http://www.census.gov/compendia/statab/cats/population/ancestry_language_spoken_at_home.html, accessed 21 November 2009.

Vasconcelos, Paula de. 1996. *Le Making of de Macbeth*. Montreal: Theatre Pigeons International.

Wakabayashi, Judy. 2005. "Translation in the East Asian Cultural Sphere: Shared Roots, Divergent Paths?" In *Asian Translation Traditions*, edited by Eva Hung and Judy Wakabayashi, 17–65. Manchester: St. Jerome.

Continentalism and the invention of traditions in translation studies

Dirk Delabastita

This theoretical case study starts from a brief critical discussion of Eurocentrism in translation studies, underscoring the importance of the efforts toward a more inclusive, truly global and culturally balanced approach to translation which are increasingly being made in our field, often under the banner of "the international turn." However, the rejection of Eurocentrism leaves open a wide range of alternative models and approaches, and this paper aims to show that the search for alternatives is not without its own difficulties. For example, it might be tempting for non-European scholars to derive an alternative way of thinking about translation from translational practices and discourses in their own continent that appear to be at odds with what is perceived as the "European" model of translation. A post-colonial sensibility would seem to make this an extremely attractive proposition. This is the line of thinking which inspired Edwin Gentzler's *Translation and Identity in the Americas. New Directions in Translation Theory* (2008). The paper enters into a critical dialogue with Gentzler's book in order to argue the general thesis that the replacement of one (perceived) continent-based paradigm by another (perceived) continent-based paradigm is not the best way forward, suffering as it does from a range of methodological problems. The best way to overcome Eurocentrism is not to construct and promote an American continentalism ("translation in the American sense") as an alternative to it, or any other nationally or continentally defined concept of translation, for that matter.

1. Eurocentrism and the international turn in translation studies

The term "Eurocentrism" is surprisingly recent but the phenomenon it names goes back a long way. Its history can perhaps be retraced as far as the Greek and Roman Empires, although it is generally believed that Eurocentrism became an important feature of Western ideologies from the Renaissance on, when the exploration and colonization of "overseas" territories began for good. It could be argued that the very belatedness of the emergence of the term is an index of the pervasive strength of Eurocentric thinking and just another example of the almost casual naturalness with which Westerners have a tendency to assume that their values, ideas and representations of the world have universal currency: being so deeply engrained in our thinking, these categories exist in mental and discursive spaces beyond critical self-scrutiny and indeed even beyond naming.[1] In the subtle way of ideologies, Eurocentrism has more to do with the categories that we think *with* than those we think *about*.

I would argue that, logically speaking, the concept of Eurocentrism breaks down into the following beliefs and convictions:

1. below the apparent variety of cultural manifestations, there is something like a common and continuous European heritage, which has its roots in the classical and Judeo-Christian traditions and developed throughout the centuries, finally articulating itself in Enlightened modern notions of freedom, democracy, organized states, rational science, technology, progress, and so on;
2. these values and achievements have given Europe a dominant place in the military, political, economic and intellectual history of the world in the past centuries;
3. Europe may safely assume that its models of the world and its value systems apply (or are waiting to be applied) elsewhere, as well;
4. in axiological terms, the European models and values are intrinsically superior to non-Western ones; in diachronic terms they are paradoxically both more ancient (i.e., original) and more modern (i.e., spearheading the future that humanity is or should be moving toward).

This working definition of Eurocentrism remains open to further debate but, even allowing for the qualifications that the definition may require, it is hard to deny that Eurocentrism should have no place in scholarly research. It involves forms of intellectual dogmatism and ethical arrogance which are difficult to reconcile with the open and critical spirit that should prevail in scholarly inquiry. In the humanities, for instance, Eurocentrism may result in the failure to even take an interest in cultural practices outside the Western context despite explicit or implicit claims to theoretical generality. Alternatively, it may entail the tendency to submit non-Western practices to Western theories in ways that fail to register and respect the formers' cultural specificity.

Translation scholars from the world over are now increasingly and quite legitimately wondering whether our current theories and methodologies in translation studies really have the "general" validity that their academic and theoretical status would imply. To what extent are the well-known translation models — say, those

---

1. Being a European myself, I am using the first person here consciously and self-critically.

discussed in Anthony Pym's *Exploring Translation Theories* (2010) — tailored to fit translational practices existing in the West only? To what extent is there an ethnocentrism at work in them which can be contested by considering the practices and theories from different parts of the world? Such critical questions are being raised more and more insistently. They follow quite logically from our growing postcolonial sensibility, the greater presence and visibility of non-Western scholars in Academia, and the overall erosion of the Western hegemony — to name but a few. Some are speaking of an "international turn" in the discipline to refer to such efforts toward a more inclusive, truly global and culturally balanced approach to translation. Important exponents of this growing movement include *Translating Others* (2 volumes), edited by Theo Hermans (2006), and Maria Tymoczko's *Enlarging Translation, Empowering Translations* (2007), as well as volumes such as *Nation and Translation in the Middle East* (Selim 2009), *Chinese Discourses on Translation. Positions and Perspectives* (Cheung 2009), *Decentering Translation Studies: India and Beyond* (Wakabayashi and Kothari 2009) and *Translation Studies in Africa* (Inggs and Meintjes 2009).

Another major exponent of the same trend is Edwin Gentzler's *Translation and Identity in the Americas* from 2008. In this well informed and engagingly written book, Gentzler explores "New Directions in Translation Theory" (the book's subtitle) by tackling "the important question of the role played by translation in the shaping of the Americas" (from Susan Bassnett's endorsement on the back cover). In what follows, I shall enter into a critical dialogue with Gentzler's book because it presents such an eloquent and powerful challenge to Eurocentrism in translation studies. I shall discuss the book in the manner of a theoretical case study. Special attention will be given to reconstructing Gentzler's response to Eurocentrism, the discursive and logical moves that drive it forwards, and the problems that it appears to run into. Even though the space afforded by a single article does not allow me fully to substantiate this claim, I believe that the following analysis of Gentzler's line of argument can be extrapolated and applied *mutatis mutandis* to other efforts that aim to challenge Eurocentrism by replacing it with another continent-based paradigm.

2. Americentrism in translation studies?

Translation and Identity in the Americas seeks to replace a "Eurocentric" model of translation with what is construed as a typically "American" one, which manifests itself in both certain practices and certain theoretical discourses on translation.[2]

---

2. Both "American" Gentzler and myself refer to the Continent as a whole and not just to the USA.

Gentzler appears to regard "European" translation theory as forming a fairly homogeneous continent-wide whole and finds it wanting. The American approach is offered as a valid alternative waiting in the wings to find its due place on the center stage of translation studies, where it can provide "new directions" for the discipline as a whole.

The book's various chapters discuss various American practices and theories that are associated with very different geographical regions and historical traditions. It successively deals with multiculturalism in the United States; feminism and theater in Quebec (Canada); cannibalism in Brazil; the fictional turn in Latin America; and border writing in the Caribbean. For each of these, a wealth of specific data and documents are presented and carefully contextualized. Different countries from the continent's north, south and middle are discussed, as well as: men and women; poets, novelists and playwrights; different languages and cultural situations; traditions and innovations.

And yet, for all its diversity, the book creates the impression that it speaks about and for the American continent *as a whole*, not in an exhaustive manner of course, but by going to the heart of several cases that are presented as *typical* of the continent. It is true that the author is always careful to use the plural — "American identities" — rather than the singular. Along the same lines Susan Bassnett argues in the Foreword that "there is no single perspective" (2008: ix). The book's central trope, however, is a metonymy that extends selected American experiences to the whole continent, endowing them with a pan-American resonance. Inasmuch as this is the case, the use of plurals is a rhetorical device camouflaging the constant pull beneath the surface of the book to put local specificities together on a single common American denominator. Thus, at the end of the chapter on the fictional turn in Latin America, Gentzler states:

> Reading Latin American fiction from the perspective of translation, I suggest, informs *our understanding* not only of the nature of translation *in the Americas*, but also of how *our identities* have been formed and will continue to be reshaped in the future. (2008: 142; italics mine)

The points made about translation in the Latin American context are presented not only as emerging from the region's particular history and cultural situation but also as being representative somehow of the Americas across the board. The conscientious use of the plural ("the Americas", "our identities") is counterbalanced and ultimately outweighed by the commonality which is created by the pronoun "our" in "our understanding" and especially "our identities" and by the projection of a single destiny for cultural identities on the continent ("will continue to be reshaped in the future"). This effect is not undone by the room for interpretive maneuver left by the periphrastic vagueness of "informs our understanding of."

The book has many extensions or extrapolations of the same type. Through their cumulative effect and the strategic position where they are often found — e.g., at the end of a section or chapter, where they acquire the decisiveness and inevitability of a logical conclusion — they enhance each other and cause the plural American perspectives to converge in a deep common sense of American identity. To support this claim I will now quote a sampling of these extrapolations, without adding further comment but italicizing the passages where the discursive shift occurs which upgrades a "regional" translational practice or discourse into a constitutive feature of the continent's cultural identity:

> In the course of this chapter, I argue that the anthropophagist translation theorists well understand the double constitution of the cannibalist metaphor and the unique cultural possibilities opened by its advocates, possibilities that allow Brazilians, *and by extension, other American subjects*, to forge their own independent cultural identities. (80)

> Cannibalism alone *unites us*. Socially. Economically. Philosophically. (81, quoted from Oswald de Andrade's "Cannibalist Manifesto" from 1928)

> Cannibalist translation, as a model of cultural evolution, can *show all Americans* a way of taking at least partial control of the construction of their own identities. (107)

> García Márquez [...] seems to be saying that translation, for all its impurities and shortcomings, is one of the keys to understanding *not just Latin America but the whole hemisphere*. (123)

> The book [Rudolfo Anaya's *Bless Me, Ultima*] holds *an uncanny resonance for Chicano as well as North American audiences*. (150)

> Thus translation is heavily tied to Gómez-Peña's conceptions of identity not just at the borders *but in the Americas in general*. (159)

> One characteristic of translation *in the Americas*, beginning with Borges [...], is that this ethic is being called into question. (164)

> As exemplified by Selvon's creative writing from the 1950s, the realization that translation is constitutive of the daily lives of its inhabitants, fundamental to their sense of identity, is particularly clear in Caribbean cultures, *yet also discernable transnationally across the borders of the nation-states of the Americas*. (168)

The pattern should be clear by now. I shall limit myself to quoting just one more example. It is of special interest inasmuch as it reveals an aporia in the author's argument:

> Translation thus ceases to be a marginal activity, and becomes an ongoing, permanent activity fundamental to the lives and the identities of the vast majority of Caribbean citizens. I suggest that this psychosocial condition in the Caribbean of always being involved in multiple processes of translation can give scholars insight into the nature of translation and identity formation *in the Americas and perhaps in other cultures worldwide as well*. (177; italics mine)

Again the extrapolation occurs which is instrumental in evoking a deep-rooted sense of pan-American identity. But this case is different because the extrapolation here overshoots itself and lands on the far side of the oceans that set off America from the rest of the world. Despite the author's hesitation ("perhaps"), we are suddenly invited to envisage cross-continental similarities far beyond what is elsewhere consistently presented as an American equation. A similar (and similarly short-lived) opening-up of perspectives occurs on page 114, where it is said that "Borges shows […] that this cannibalist tradition is not limited to Latin America but present in European translation traditions as well." Why not zoom out and start investigating whether the translational practices and discourses that are claimed to be characteristic of the Americas may not be found outside the continent as well?

As we have just seen, translation is described as a "permanent activity fundamental to the lives and the identities of [a] vast majority of citizens" in the Caribbean and more broadly "in the Americas" (177). But, to be sure, it is not hard to find situations in "other cultures worldwide as well," far beyond the Americas, where such a situation applies. Quite ironically, one example that may well spring to mind is that of the various communities permanently trying to find their own voice and sense of self in a multilingual, multi-ethnic and translation-based place like Brussels — the administrative and proverbial heart of Europe! Countless other cases could be quoted ranging from Hong Kong to South Africa with its eleven officially recognized languages, of which one — English — is nevertheless becoming more hegemonic. Discussing the general situation of African authors, Paul Bandia notes that they can be viewed as "both translators and translated beings [and] their bilingual existence can be seen as an embodiment of translation" (Bandia 2009: 15). They seek to assert their "cultural heritage" and "affirm their difference" by deploying "innovative linguistic strategies" (ibid.). Doesn't this invite comparison with the Americas?

It would be poor scholarship to allow our comparative zest to erase the differences between these and other cultural situations across the globe, but it remains striking that *Translation and Identity in the Americas* is reluctant to address the possibility that certain translational realities from the Americas may well have analogues and counterparts in other parts of the world and that the book remains silent on the need for wide-angle comparative research to investigate this hypothesis. The reason for this disinclination is not hard to fathom. The book posits the deep-seated existence of a translation-based identity for the continent as a whole. The sheer possibility that the modes and modalities of "typically" American translation may exist elsewhere in more or less comparable forms would fatally dilute this alleged American identity and thus weaken the book's underlying thesis. Clearly, it is a possibility best not contemplated, let alone investigated by promoting international comparative research.

We could question the validity of Gentzler's extrapolations not only on account of the abruptness with which they end at America's shores but also for the ease with which, having started in one region of America, they sweep across the whole continent. Specific American realities are extended to become typical American realities. But can we avoid raising the issue of the representativeness of the corpus of American realities that is highlighted in *Translation and Identity in the Americas*? A very diverse selection of translation practices and discourses is discussed, but to what extent can they stand for the continent as a whole? In other words, how much statistical tweaking or symbolic distortion is implicitly involved in the critical maneuver which gives a pan-American significance to, say, Quebec feminism or Latin American translation fictions? This issue is conspicuously absent from the book's agenda. The extrapolations occur smoothly and discretely, with no hard questions asked. It turns out that an overwhelming amount of attention is devoted to the practices and views of certain relatively small avant-garde groups and intellectual elites and, conversely, that comparatively scant attention is devoted to how most ordinary folk up and down the continent deal with language, multilingualism and translation in their neighborhoods, at school, on radio and television, on their PCs and smartphones, in movie theaters, in magazines and in mainstream book publishing, let alone in a range of professional settings.[3] Even if the systematic research remains to be done, it is hard to believe that it would be standard practice across the Americas for translators to engage in "transgressive" translation and to relish "the risk of adding phonetic, syntactic, and/or semantic connotations that resonate differently and highly creatively in the target culture" (97). For a start, such a belief would be hard to square with the dominance of the regime of fluency in the English-speaking world as famously described and denounced by Lawrence Venuti in his *The Translator's Invisibility* (1995).

The reluctance to construe "American" translation views and practices in a broader comparative perspective beyond the geographical limits of America is thus matched by a reluctance to consider the representativeness of these same views and practices within the confines of the American continent. But then, these

---

3. A similar assessment is expressed by some of the critics quoted in the book, Roberto Schwartz and Sérgio Bellei. Both writers present a "critique of the 'elitist' nature of the De Campos brothers' theories of translation" (p. 104).

avant-garde translation practices and discourses seem to have been selected — to the exclusion of so much else within and outside the continent — because they show certain similarities and because their perceived convergence enables an American concept of translation to be born. That is the point I will argue in the next section.

3. American identities

It is often the case that the observer of a cultural identity and tradition ends up getting entangled in its construction, tacitly moving from observation to participation. It seems that *Translation and Identity in the Americas* presents an example of this mechanism. Gentzler is not merely charting the emergence or the existence of a translation-based American cultural identity, but he is also actively engaged in its construction or invention. That is why the title of this paper alludes to Eric Hobsbawm and Terence Ranger's classic volume from 1983: *The Invention of Tradition*. The construction and propagation of this American cultural identity happen through a narrative involving three closely intertwined storylines.

The first storyline is that American translators have come to reject the insipid European ethos of passive recreation, submission and invisibility; they claim equal freedom and status for their texts as originals. In other words, the American translator stands up against the tyranny of the source text which typically keeps European translators enslaved:

> Translation for De Campos [...] is more similar to original writing, just as inventive, spontaneous, and irreverent. The goal is a re-version, a reinvention, of the source text, reconstituting the movement of signs in one multilingual culture in another, equally multilingual culture, transcreating the original. (97)

> Translation in the American sense is a bold genre. (186)

The second storyline involves America rejecting the dominance and supposed superiority of Europe, which it still perceives as its symbolic colonizer. In other words, the (colonized) continent stands up against its (former) Master Europe:

> Brazil, implies Augusto de Campos, discovers its identity not in the similarity of its artistic ideas and expressions to those of the European masters but in the differences of its ideas and expressions. (99)

> Borges's clever story [...] contains a parody of traditional translation studies, Eurocentric literary histories, Arabic studies in Germany, and institutions of literary authority. Extended interpretations also allow for seeing it as a Latin American rebellion against the colonizing European monarchies. (115)

The two storylines come together where American translators engage in creatively subversive translations of European texts with transgressive translation becoming a defiant act of counter-European self-affirmation:

> [A] classic of Western literature is read and rewritten from the perspective of the Americas. The result is the construction of a powerful metaphor for translation, or, perhaps better said, mistranslation and resistance. (172)

> [T]he use of foreign models is not a passive, derivative activity [...] Cuban writers are open to the creative possibilities inherent in translation [...] Translation in the traditional European sense is a timid genre, showing one's dependence upon European literary forms and ideas; translation in the Cuban Caribbean sense is a resistant genre, showing one's independence from European forms and leading to new and highly original styles. (175)

The third storyline shows that the aforementioned two movements are also reflected at the level of scholarly discourses, where they entail a "refusal [...] to adopt a model of translation preferred by European culture" (102). Thus, a new and specifically American brand of translation theory is seen emerging which is post-nationalist, allows for creativity, freedom and change, and has a living relationship with translation practice. It asserts itself against traditional translation theory, which is essentially European, preoccupied with national languages and national literary canons, and entertaining naïve ideas about universality and the reproducibility of identical meanings. Here is some textual evidence:

> Translation is [...] seen as a site of tension between Europe and the Americas, with not only the authority of the source text being called into question but also the very model for the study of translation. (102)

> The idea that the translation changes the original is sacrilegious to not only traditional (and many contemporary) translation studies scholars but also, more importantly, those European critics and cultural institutions who defend the sanctity of the existing canon — the great books — and the authors who write them. (133–134)

> [O]ne borderline [Derrida] wishes to distinguish is that between translation studies governed by classical models of translation — one that assumes national languages and a kind of universality achievable through the translatability of that language into other national languages — and a translation studies that challenges and destructures such notions — one that embraces multilingual reference, polysemia, and dissemination. (171)

> I suggest that translation studies scholars in the Americas are increasingly viewing translation less as a rhetorical form aimed at accessing some unified original essence than as a discursive practice that reveals multiple signs of the heterogeneous and polyvalent nature of the construction of culture. (183)

The subtext that I have highlighted in the preceding paragraphs leaves much of Edwin Gentzler's lively narrative untold. But that subtext is unmistakably present in the book, providing a powerful undercurrent to the many strands of its complex argument, and doing so in a very persuasive manner, too. Given the reputation of its author and the impact of the book's publisher (Routledge), this intervention in the debate on the international theme in translation studies is bound to be a significant one on American campuses and far beyond. That is why it deserves further scrutiny.

4.   Further complications

"Translation in the American sense" (186) is not a reality that offers itself to the observer; it is primarily a reality that has been constructed discursively by selecting certain views and practices and configuring them in such a way as to flag up both their mutual affinities and their contrast with the otherness of what is allegedly the European tradition. Such a construction comes at a cost. We have already pointed out that it raises thorny issues of representativeness and typicality both within and outside the American continent.

But more questions arise. Thus, one is led to wonder how relevant the *geographically* based idea of continents can be relevant to a *cultural* analysis to begin with. It may be an interesting working hypothesis to say that the American continent has something like a translation-based cultural identity which is strongly marked by the emancipation from (past) colonization by Europe. But as a hypothesis this assumption would need to be tested rather than demonstrated, and in doing so the opposition between "us" and "them" ("European" versus "American") is surely too blunt as an analytical tool. We need to remind ourselves of a few basic facts. Colonization, post-colonial movements and tensions between centers and peripheries occur and have occurred *within* Europe, too. They have also occurred within the Americas. They seem to be a recurrent feature of human history worldwide and it may be useful to recall that American nations too have been actively engaged in colonial or imperialistic projects abroad, with or without the complicity of certain European nations (which evokes the quite fundamental complication of the unclear relationship between "Europe" and the "Western world"!). And last but not least, an increasing amount of discursive and translational activity is now taking place in cyberspace, in globalized forums and decision-making bodies and in other intercontinental or delocalized settings which make the traditional political or geographical borders of nations and continents look like archaeological traces from a previous epoch. Pitting one continent against another can hardly offer the fine-grained analysis that is required to map this complex and multilayered landscape with its rapidly changing positions and power differentials.

Another unresolved issue is that the American voices in translation theory as heard, quoted and paraphrased by Edwin Gentzler are so intensely resonant with the echoes of Parisian intellectuals, showing a strong "similarity of [their] ideas and expressions to those of the European masters" (99). French post-structuralism and Derrida especially (e.g., 9–10, 27, 29–31, 68–72, 92–96, 130, 134–137, 144, 149, 168–171, 187, and so on) are omnipresent. The author's articulation of the common American denominator seems to require the intellectual input of various Europeans or thinkers belonging to the European tradition.[4] It is deeply ironic that this dependency on European sources presents a repeat of the old colonial situation which the author is so keen to critique in his bid to define identity in the Americas. Referring to the apparent relevance of Gayatri Spivak's work for border writing and translation, Gentzler rightly notes the "uneasiness among Latin American scholars about replacing one kind of political colonialism with a kind of intellectual imperialism" (145). But doesn't his overall dependence on French post-structuralism place him in a similar position of self-imposed intellectual compliance with the old European center?

In a number of instances Gentzler is able to demonstrate that certain Western or European views were already anticipated, or have autonomous homologues, in the Americas, or even that Europeans were enriched and inspired by what they saw in the Americas. For instance:

> [Brazilian] writers have arrived at a theory of translation and identity formation that is historically rich, culturally diverse, and theoretically highly original, anticipating many of the debates characteristic of critical theory in the West today. (79–80)

> This work in the Caribbean and Latin America predated the most widely known theorist of hybridity in translation studies circles, Homi Bhabha. (144–145)

Showing an uncanny resemblance with the claims of Eurocentrism that its views are paradoxically both more ancient and more modern (see Section 1 above), the American views on translation, culture and identity are presented as simultaneously having a long tradition and being capable of showing the "new directions" for the future of translation studies. These are most interesting points, but are they sufficient to dispel the strong sense of dependence on Parisian intellectuals? Who derives credibility from whom? And what would Derrida himself have

---

4. The issue is actually more complicated: a striking number of European/Western intellectuals that are quoted with approval are of Jewish origin: Andrew Benjamin, Walter Benjamin, Hélène Cixous, Jacques Derrida, Franz Kafka. As such, they are hardly typical Europeans; they know everything about borders, migration, translation and identity. Some would argue that they can be seen as victims of Europe rather than as representatives of it.

made of Gentzler's search for origins or, for that matter, of the author's recourse to "older distinctions" and "binary oppositions" of which he otherwise advocates their deconstruction: "source/target, home/foreign, original/translation, colonial/postcolonial" (145)?

My last question bears on the ambivalent status of *Translation and Identity in the Americas* as a contribution to translation research. We have already alluded several times to the book's subtitle: *New Directions in Translation Theory*, but the exact significance of this phrase — and especially of the word "theory" — never becomes entirely clear. The book shows very convincingly that translation-wise fascinating things are happening on the American continent. Gentzler takes us on a captivating trip, revealing some very creative translation practices and introducing us to challenging and often beautifully expressed views and discourses *on* translation by poets, dramatists, novelists and translators. But what is the scholarly status of these translational practices and poetic or fictional discourses on translation? Sometimes it is stated or implied that they *are* or *constitute* theories, indeed taking translation theory in a new direction: e.g., "translation is increasingly used to articulate a new theory of culture" (60); "translation becomes a place for theorizing aspects of minority practices" (32); "West Indian writing/translation is more than a theoretical idea" (175); "the theory [...] is articulated [...] more via a creative discursive practice" (177); and so on. Sometimes they appear in the book as a "theory", but with the word qualified by scare quotes: e.g., "color is the main way Brossard thematizes translation, and herein lies the writing/translation 'theory'" (64). In still other cases they are *not* presented as theories, either with or without distancing scare quotes, but merely as empirical realities that can inspire or prompt a new kind of translation theory which is still waiting to be fully developed: "have repercussions for translation theory" (145); "engendered theories of translation" (109); "can inform [...] translation theory" (110), "the discourse of fiction [...] used as a source for theories about translation" (136).

One senses an ambiguity here concerning the relationship between historical practice and theoretical discourse, and between artistic/creative discourses on translation and scholarly ones. As a scholar, I wish that Gentzler had been more outspoken as to whether it is possible and/or desirable to make a distinction between theories that are "scholarly" (explicit, research-based, methodologically grounded) and those that are less or not at all scholarly (and which would thus belong to the scholars' field of investigation rather than to their theoretical toolkit). If we accept that the line between scholarly discourses and non-scholarly discourses about translation is often difficult to draw, would that, in the author's opinion, also mean that the distinction is meaningless and not even worth trying to make? In his 1928 *Cannibalist Manifesto* Oswald de Andrade proudly affirms that he has "never permitted the birth of logic" among his group (qtd. in Gentzler 2008:81).

Such a position is legitimate in itself and exactly the kind of thing one expects from poets. But when Gentzler embraces these views and the epistemology they embody, where does that leave his book as a contribution to translation studies understood as an academic and research-based discipline? While the interest of the cannibalist theory of translation is never at stake, how can one claim it to offer a viable conceptual model that could guide us in our scholarly work?

The bottom line of this series of questions is this: for how much should rational logic count in our theory-building and our scholarly work more generally? This is a pressing question because those who believe in good old logic may be disconcerted to see that many of the "new directions in translation theory" are given by intellectuals who are positively averse to it. Suzanne Jill Levine, Luce Irigaray, Barbara Goddard, Jacques Derrida and other favorites of Gentzler dislike linear thinking and mistrust the kind of theory that produces the "harsh and brutal [...] light of midday" (65) and leads to "final logical solutions" (68). Clearly, the author does not feel comfortable with theory that is articulated "in a logical, European, descriptive fashion" (177). But is it fair to suggest that rigorous logic and descriptive aspirations would be the exclusive domain of European thinkers and scientists? And isn't the phrase "final logical solutions" thoroughly misleading with its verbal echo of the *Endlösung* of the Nazis? And why would a rigorous sense of logic always have to lead to firm conclusions (unlike ideology, logic tends to generate more questions than answers)?

Concluding remarks

Translation and Identity in the Americas is an informative and well written book. It covers an impressive range of challenging texts and ideas with insight and a fine sense of historical context, containing some splendid passages of literary criticism as well. Yet, I cannot but disagree with Edwin Gentzler's grand narrative which writes off "European" approaches to translation and replaces them by an "American" set of translational ideas and practices. Inasmuch as Eurocentrism is a problem in translation studies, it will first of all need to be identified more accurately before it can be addressed. Whatever the expected outcome of this exercise, the best way to overcome Eurocentrism is not to promote American continentalism as an alternative to it — or Sinocentrism or Afrocentrism or any other form of nationally or continentally defined ethnocentrism, for that matter. As my critical dialogue with *Translation and Identity in the Americas* has hopefully demonstrated, such an approach involves a range of methodological, logical and epistemological shortcuts and problems. Quite ironically, it can even be seen as perpetuating the Eurocentrism it had wished to confront.

The challenge for translation studies in this global age is much tougher. It ought to develop a framework of concepts and models that makes it possible to deal with the worldwide variety of cultural situations and their interrelatedness in a truly comparative way (for my own modest effort to that end, see Delabastita 2008). This requires that a delicate balance be struck between two imperatives. On the one hand, the model needs to possess sufficient generality and descriptive precision to serve as a global research platform. On the other hand, this should not prevent the translation scholar from developing the empathy and the local affinities needed to capture the specifics of individual cultural realities. Edwin Gentzler's continentalist project shows much of the latter but rather too little of the former, illustrating just how difficult it is to get the balance right.

References

Bandia, Paul. 2009. "Translation Matters: Linguistic and Cultural Representation." In *Translation Studies in Africa*, edited by Judith Inggs and Libby Meintjes, 1–20. London/New York: Continuum.

Cheung, Martha P. (ed.). 2006. *An Anthology of Chinese Discourse of Translation. Volume 1. From Earliest Times to the Buddhist Project*. Manchester: St Jerome.

Cheung, Martha P. (ed.). 2009. *Chinese Discourses on Translation. Positions and Perspectives*. Special issue of *The Translator* 15.2.

Delabastita, Dirk. 2008. "Status, Origin, Features." In *Beyond Descriptive Translation Studies. Investigations in Homage to Gideon Toury*, edited by Anthony Pym, Miriam Shlesinger and Daniel Simeoni, 233–246. Amsterdam/Philadelphia: John Benjamins.

Gentzler, Edwin. 2008. *Translation and Identity in the Americas. New Directions in Translation Theory*. London/New York: Routledge.

Hobsbawm, Eric and Terence Ranger (eds.). 1983. *The Invention of Tradition*. Cambridge: Cambridge University Press.

Inggs, Judith and Libby Meintjes (eds.). 2009. *Translation Studies in Africa*. London/New York: Continuum.

Selim, Samah (ed.). 2009. *Nation & Translation in the Middle East* (special issue of *The Translator* 15:1). Manchester: St Jerome.

Tymoczko, Maria. 2009. *Enlarging Translation, Empowering Translators*. Manchester/Kinderhook: St Jerome.

Venuti, Lawrence. 1995. *The Translator's Invisibility: A History of Translation*. London: Routledge.

Wakabayashi, Judy and Kothari, Rita (eds.). 2009. *Decentering Translation Studies: India and Beyond*. Amsterdam/Philadelphia: John Benjamins.

How Eurocentric is Europe?

Examining scholars' and translators' contributions to translation studies — an ethnographic perspective

Peter Flynn

Conceptualizations of translation are often cast in the literature in terms of sets of hegemonic dualities played out across lines of continuous and perhaps irresolvable dominance and resistance in all areas touched on by translation: language, power, ethnicity, gender, etc. This paper will attempt to trace trajectories of thought and inquiry within Translation Studies in order to discover to which extent certain approaches and models can be considered (strictly) as Western, Eurocentric and hence as propagating a priori such power and other imbalances. In this respect, the article argues for a situated approach to understanding the use of certain analytical concepts in given cultural spaces. It further argues that concepts and models be viewed in combination and in contrast with ethnographic studies of translation practices. It therefore asserts that translational practices should be explored on the ground in order to complement and adjust scholarly conceptualizations of translation in the broadest sense. Ethnographic studies of the field allow us to discover the impact of practices on (or in the construction of) a given cultural space or on other practices visible in the same space. This further helps us explore differences between these practices, along with their theoretical underpinnings, and those held by scholars in the same space. Data drawn from an ethnographic study of literary translators in the Netherlands and Belgium will be used to discuss some of the points outlined above.

Introduction

This paper will pursue and try to bring together two strands of inquiry. First, it will attempt to disambiguate perceptions within the literature in which conceptualizations of translation are often cast in terms of sets of hegemonic dualities played out across lines of continuous and perhaps irresolvable dominance and resistance in all areas touched on by translation: language, power, ethnicity, gender, etc. By tracing trajectories of thought and inquiry within Translation Studies, it will ask to what extent certain approaches and models can be labelled as Western, Eurocentric, resistant or other. Second, it will advocate situated inquiries into such trajectories in combination with ethnographic studies of translation practices. In this respect, it asserts that translational practices should be explored on the ground in order to complement and adjust scholarly conceptualizations of translation in the broadest sense. In lieu of casting translators' practices and positions in the mold of hegemonic academic discourse and framing them in terms of resistance to extant academic models, it is further suggested that no adequate theory of translation can be posited without also theorizing the roles, actions, and discourses of translators as such. Following a preliminary discussion of the literature, each strand of inquiry will be tackled separately below, followed by a conclusion that will attempt to bring the two strands together.

It is a truism or perhaps an old chestnut to argue that there would be no Translation Studies without translations. An obvious corollary to this truism is that there would be no translations and hence no Translation Studies without translators (among others). Whereas the truism can be accepted at its face value, the corollary brings various difficulties with it and begs one important question: how do/can we "theorize" translators? Since the late 1990s, Translation Studies has shown a clear interest in translators, their practices and discourses. This is visible in studies on translation history and sociology: Gouanvic 1997; Pym 1998; Wolf & Fukari (eds.), 2007; Pym, Shlesinger & Jettmarova (eds.) 2003, inter alia; and in work based on Bourdieu's concepts of practice, habitus and field: Simeoni 1998; Inghilleri 2003; Gouanvic 2005; Sela-Sheffy 2006, among many others. These studies were preceded by research into norms drawing on Toury (1995) and Chesterman (1993), norms being what Pym called "an eminently sociological concept" (Pym 2003: 3)

More recently, researchers have been using ethnographic approaches to study translator's and interpreters' practices (Angelelli 2004; Koskinen 2008, to name but two). Such studies also coincide with work by translation scholars examining the translation practices and related ideological underpinnings of ethnographers as translators, both in classical and more recent ethnographies (Sturge 1997, 2007; Bachmann-Medick 2006). Like Pym (1998), these scholars went in search of translators or interpreters (note the plural).Their hypostatic singularly inert counterpart "the translator" can be inserted easily into any translation model. The plural, on the other hand, brings with it a whole range of "subjective," and inter-subjective real-world practices and discourses that frighten and bedevil model builders.

Within literary translation, this problem has generally, though not always, been tackled on a case by case basis. Each case often addresses individual translators or movements that have gained a public face and subsequently an iconic status through their translation work, as well as through their (theoretical and/or experienced-based) writings/discourses on translation, e.g., those discussed in Robinson (2002) or Cheung (2006), or within other regional or national contexts. For the Dutch-language area, contemporary translators and/or authors such as Paul Claes, Frans Denissen, Peter Verstegen and others come to mind. The impact these translators have had on translation studies is not to be underestimated, Walter Benjamin being an illustrious case in point.

In a certain sense, Gentzler's recent work, *Translation and Identity in the Americas* continues this tradition by exploring the work of individual translators/writers or "schools" of or movements in translation within the Americas (viz. *réécriture au feminin* in Canada (Gentzler 2008: 40–76); *movimento antropófago* in Brazil (Gentzler 2008: 77–107), etc.) and their innovative ways of conceptualizing translation and the consequences these conceptualizations have for the discipline of Translation Studies (Gentzler 2008). The schools explored in Gentzler's work are situated in broader cultural movements and often viewed in terms of their resistance to dominant or hegemonic "Western" or (neo)colonialist or neo-nationalist cultural practices.

That these people deserve attention and praise is beyond question, but perhaps it is not unimportant to note in the context of this article that the step from their translation practices to the articulation/theorization of these practices in academic discourse is sometimes a very short one, as many of those involved are important cultural presences, have close ties with the world of academia, and are theorists and/or lecturers themselves (viz. Augusto de Campos, Annie Brisset, Suzanne Jill Levine, among others). In the case of other lesser known translators, one can ask how these articulation and theorization processes have been facilitated and also how certain translator/theorists have managed to open the door to academic acceptance, finding their way more easily than others into scholarly works. Such acceptance implies visibility and raises with it the question of what visibility or invisibility consists in (Venuti 1995, Simeoni 1998). Much depends on who is watching and whether or not the observed wish to be seen in the first place and, if so, how they wish to be seen or represented.

In this respect, an attempt will be made below to illustrate briefly how many other translators operating below the horizon of academic visibility have equally insightful things to say about their practices and to share with translation scholars. Like the translators who have become visible to the discipline, they, too, are worth listening to. The broader question of how they and their practices should be theorized remains open, however, and needs to be examined in concordance with the ideas of more visible translators, i.e., those who have achieved recognition within the discipline through references in scholarly articles and books. Before discussing the contributions of these less visible translators, we will first trace a couple of trajectories of thought in Translation Studies as such and attempt to argue for a more situated — and paradoxically de-westernised — understanding of concepts and models in the discipline.

1.   Trajectories of thought

In pursuing trajectories of thought, another point worth mentioning regarding Gentzler's recent work and the general debate on "de-westernizing" translation studies concerns the presence therein, both real and in terms of translation theory, of certain "Western," if not European, thinkers (cf. Benjamin, Berman, Cixous, Derrida, Eagleton, Foucault, among others). This alone calls into question what is meant by (outmoded) Western or European translation models. Should the terms "Western" and "Euro-centric" be only understood along the lines set out in Tymoczko (2009), where they are used as shorthand for everything obsolete, narrowly linguistic and deserving of rejection? Tymoczko points out herself that "[a] t this point in time, however, when Western ideas have permeated the world and there is widespread interpenetration of cultures everywhere, the terms east and west become increasingly problematic" (Tymoczko 2005: 1n).

Her call for a "de-westernising" of translation studies (Tymoczko 2009: 403), though noble in intent, fails to take into account the influence of Western forms of thinking underlying the call. In a related vein, a clear line of thought can also be traced from French Poststructuralism to Cultural Studies to Translation Studies, visible, among others things, in the influence of Derrida on prominent North American translation scholars such as Lawrence Venuti. But this is most probably not the type of Westernism or Euro-centrism that is being alluded to.

The profound influence (through translation) of thinkers and language scholars from Eastern Europe like Bakhtin and Voloshinov on French Poststructuralism is undeniable, stemming from a time when these scholars lay far beyond the pale of "Western" or even "European, i.e., Western European," scholarship. As a result one might ask: how French is French Poststructuralism? On this side of the Atlantic, other French scholars like Pierre Bourdieu, whose work has also had undeniable impact on Translation Studies and especially the sociology of (literary) translation (viz. Gouanvic 2007) mainly though not entirely in Europe (viz. also Simeoni 1998 on translational habitus), were quick to acknowledge the importance of American scholars such as Goffman and Labov (Bourdieu 2001: 200–1) when it came to the study of language and social interaction:

Dans cette perspective, la politique de traduction était un élément capital: je pense par exemple à Labov dont l'œuvre et la présence active ont servi de base au développement en France d'une vraie sociolinguistique, renouant avec la tradition européenne dont il était lui même issu.

[In this perspective the politics of translation played a vital role: I am thinking for example of Labov whose work and active presence served as a basis for the development of real sociolinguistics in France, renewing the link with the European tradition from which he himself had stemmed. (translation mine)]

It seems obvious that there is more to all this than meets the eye and that it would be better to talk in terms of dialectic interaction and mutual exchange rather than rigid dichotomies cast in terms of dominance and resistance or pre and post whatever. The following examples of exchanges of thought should further illustrate the point.

1.1 The travels of concepts and approaches

The term "thick translation" has enjoyed much critical attention since it was coined by the Ghanaian scholar Kwame Appiah (Appiah 1993, Appiah in Venuti 2000). The term has been used by a number of scholars to express a variety of highly useful critical reflections on translation in a number of areas: in heightening translators' awareness of cultural differences (Appiah himself), as a critique of Western translation theoretical concepts, among other things (Hermans 2003), on feminist approaches to translation (Massardier-Kenney 1997; Wolf 2003), on rendering Chinese translation concepts in English (Cheung 2007). These authors provide the source from which the concept of "thick translation" was derived, i.e., the American anthropologist Clifford Geertz's take on the English philosopher Gilbert Ryle's notion of "thick description" (Geertz 1973: 3–30), and it may be the case that, as a philosopher, Appiah borrowed the term directly from Ryle. As far as translation studies is concerned, it remains to be discovered which scholar has been most influential in spreading the notion of "thick translation." Is it Appiah himself or Lawrence Venuti, who published Appiah's influential essay in the *Translation Studies Reader* (Venuti 2000), or the Belgian scholar Theo Hermans, who has lectured worldwide, worked as a professor of Translation Studies in China, and has also served as an editor of a number of important works on translation by internationally renowned scholars (e.g., *Crosscultural Transgressions*, 2002 and the two volumes of *Translating Others*, 2006)?

Another perhaps less obvious example is that of translation(al) competence, first suggested, as far as I am aware, by Michael Canale (Canale 1983) and now of common currency in translator training (references would be too numerous to list here). The concept is derived from communicative competence and more specifically from the seminal article by Dell Hymes, the eminent American anthropologist and sociolinguist (Hymes 1971). An examination of Hymes's views on communicative competence and a comparison with Canale's model for language and translation pedagogy shows that models undergo transformations and adjustments when they are taken up in other academic disciplines. The same reflection can be made for "thick translation" in its various guises and even "thick description" itself on its journey from philosophy to anthropology.[1] Do these concepts still mean exactly the same thing or were they ever so narrowly defined or the sole property of a given national or regional school of thought from the outset?

Likewise and perhaps more importantly, is doing "thick translation" in Ghana the same as doing "thick translation" in China? Or are such concepts not subject to local reconceptualization and recontextaulization practices (Silverstein and Urban 1996) that "de-center" them and other concepts de facto? It is suggested here that concepts like "thick translation" do not merely frame the object of study in some universal cognitive sense but are equally framed by it by being forced to engage with the situated contingencies specific to the socio-cultural space under investigation. Hence, although ostensibly the purpose here, it may prove in one sense to be a fruitless exercise to trace concepts back to their supposed origins as this desire for the comfort of beginnings would clearly obscure the situated meanings such concepts take on in their travels.

In this sense, one might ask what indeed remains of "Western" or "Euro-centric" concepts once im/exported elsewhere? Can we always assume that, in a similar vein to the ghost of corporate capitalism perhaps, they propagate and maintain some sort of nefarious skeletal cognitive superstructure that continues to frame local transformations? Could they not, perhaps paradoxically, also help fire resistant transformations and hence unintentionally subvert themselves? To use a pertinent example discussed in Kiberd (1995: 137), Daniel O'Connell's perhaps incongruous insistence during the nineteenth century on conducting the political debate in English and not in Gaelic — so that the English would understand it — did lay the foundations for later independence from Britain.

I would argue here that the rationale underlying such notions as "Western" and "Euro-centric" is that their meaning is indeed fixed, not as indicators of geographical location, but rather as metaphors and metonyms for regimes of dominance and oppression. Alas, there never has been a pristine beginning or Eden

---

1. Another interesting case in point is the influence of Indian philosophy on Ralph Waldo Emerson's thinking and its subsequent influence on Gandhi's: this example is borrowed from the paper "Translation and World Literature" given by Harish Trivedi at *The Known Unknowns of Translation Studies, International Conference in Honour of the Twentieth Anniversary of* CETRA *and* Target (1989–2009) K.U.Leuven, 28–29 August 2009.

on either side of dominance or resistance, and Europe too has its fair share of oppressed minorities, past and present. This should not be understood as an attempt to deny the oppression meted out by former European empires but rather to stress that oppression is not exclusively European, Western or imperial but shape-shifts in the same way the relation between language and meaning does. Used as shorthand terms for such regimes of dominance, "Euro-centric" and "Western" may obscure or be used to obfuscate other orders of dominance and oppression. The anti-British rhetoric pervasive in post-independence Ireland is a case in point.

Another example involves the critique of linguistic approaches to translation studies following the cultural turn (Tymoczko & Gentzler 2002: xv–xvi; Snell-Hornby 2006: 47–67). This critique, justifiable though it was in highlighting neglected areas of attention in Translation Studies, often viewed linguistics in a very narrow, obsolete sense and also as being emblematically European at that, and failed to see many of the questions addressed by linguists and the many developments within the discipline that could be used to debunk such arguments. The targets of criticism most cited are the European obsession with equivalence (cf. Werner Koller's typology of equivalence (Koller 1976) for example) and the work of such scholars as Catford, among others. Such linguistic approaches have become synonymous with or were emblematic of "Euro-centrism" and as such needed no further proof or re-examination save preliminary gesturing toward their obsolescence in comparison with the ideas and analyses to be presented in a given article. With time, such gestures became formulaic rather than challenging. Who would doubt that linguistic approaches are insufficient in addressing translation in its totality? But can any approach address translation in its totality or should it? This debate was tackled comprehensively by (the — should I say? — British scholar) Mona Baker (Baker 2001), and much of what she said back then has been further validated.

Furthermore, the earlier criticism of linguistics and comparative linguistics has not prevented scholars from using innovative linguistic approaches to translation and with considerable result; Baker's work on translation corpora is a case in point. Neither does the use of linguistic approaches to translation prevent one from being aware of cultural difference and regimes of dominance. A fine example of this is Maryns's study of asylum seeker procedures in Belgium (Maryns 2006) which draws on the work of such American anthropologists, discourse and conversation analysts and sociolinguists as Hymes, Gumperz and Ochs, among others. Perhaps the rejection/criticism of any given approach to Translation Studies should not be understood as rejection or criticism of an approach as such but rather in terms of the often polemical nature of academic discourse (see Snell-Hornby 2006: 46, for example), which in turn mirrors positionings and loyalties within subsections of the discipline, more specifically the subsections not being criticized (Bourdieu 2001: 123–141).

It is not my purpose to provide an exhaustive list of trajectories of thought in Translation Studies. The point being made here is twofold. First, it is argued that an examination of trajectories can help disambiguate dichotomous conceptualizations of Translations Studies and help point to the situated understanding and use of concepts and models in given (national/regional/local/virtual) contexts. Second, it is argued that such concepts and approaches, be they dominant, resistant or otherwise, are not just (obsolete/innovative) tools for tackling the 'raw material' of translation wherever in the world; they also play an important role in constructing, cordoning off and gate-keeping subsections of the discipline of Translation Studies itself. It is not the purpose here to discredit such practices but merely to point out that they do exist. Perhaps the idea of "turns" in translation can be understood in a similar way. As such, "turn" may create the false illusion that some sort of teleology or Kuhnian paradigm shift is involved whereby each turn supersedes the previous, now obsolete one. Clearly this is not the sole dynamic visible in Translation Studies. Having outlined trajectories of concepts within Translation Studies, I will now turn to those found in the discourse of practicing translators.

2.   Trajectories of practice and related discourse

Individual translators have over the years developed what could be called situated theories or models of translation through their engagement with their own translation work and have hence contributed to emergent ideas in Translation Studies (Benjamin, Holmes, among many others). In what follows, we will turn our attention to discourses and practices of lesser known literary translators, characterized by a richness of reflection and situated theorizing.

The data examined and discussed in what follows was collected during an ethnographic study (completed in 2005) of 12 literary translators working in the Netherlands and Flanders and provides ample evidence of this richness. The study comprised in-depth interviews (in Dutch) with the translators, observations made during a collaborative project, as well as a corpus analysis of their work (Flynn 2006). One of the research criteria was that the translator had translated Irish poetry (written in English) into Dutch, which seriously reduced the number of eligible candidates. This, of course, raises questions of how representative such a study might be of the positionings of all literary translators working in the same space, but such questions would do nothing to detract from the importance of the translation work carried out by those who participated in the study.

An analysis of the data threw up four major themes, emerging in particular from the richly layered narratives related during the interviews, which went far beyond the responses to the basic questions I posed regarding their career choices, translation practices and their relations with others in the field. These four themes were/are:

1. Professional Ethos (their engagement with texts, other colleagues, codes of professional practice, etc.);
2. Ideologies of Language (their views on historical languages, dialects, including their form, substance and functions, etc.);
3. Perceptions of Genre (how to do types of literature (in translation));
4. Perceptions of Culture (literature as culture, as cultural artefacts and as reflections, refractions of certain cultural practices and spaces).

These themes ran through all of the interviews and co-occurred in numerous utterances. As there is too little space here to discuss and illustrate these themes in great detail, I will focus on one extract from the data and further provide a table below of related central metaphors and metonyms found in the discourse of other interviewees. This extract is highly illustrative of the stances and themes found throughout the whole study and, among other things, can be used to indicate the translator's views on genre. It has been selected here mainly for its relevance to one of the main topics of this paper, namely situated understandings and uses of concepts and approaches. These concepts are usually expressed in terms of metaphors and metonyms, as the extract illustrates:

> QB1
> PF: en dus om over te gaan naar het vertalen zelf, (ja, as such, ja) ja Hoe doe je dat? Hoe begint dat? (ja)
> [And now to move on to translation itself (yes, as such, yes) yes, how do you go about it? How does it begin?]
> Reply B1
> JE:[2] Nou op een gegeven ogenblik lees ik iets van een bepaalde dichter en denk ik "dat wil ik hebben, dat is voor mij".
> [Now at a given moment I read something by a certain poet and I think "I want that, that's for me."]
> Het is een soort kannibalisme je, je vreet het op en je maakt een vertaling van en ook wil je het aan een andere laten zien "kijk eens wat mooi" zo.
> [It's a type of cannibalism, you, you devour it and you translate it and then you want to show it to everyone "look now, how beautiful it is," that sort of thing.]
> En dan begin ik daaraan en ik heb ook de gewoonte als vertaler wordt je altijd ingepeperd door mensen die wetenschappelijk mee bezig zijn die moet eerst het hele werk lezen en dan pas ga je beginnen. Maar ik begin eerst omdat ik het avontuur wil vast houden. Ja, de spanning moet er in blijven.

---

2. It must be pointed out here that the translator speaking in this extract translated a number of major works of English poetry into Dutch, including Walcott's Omeros.

[And then I get started on it and as a translator I have a habit … people who are involved with this "scientifically" are always trying to pepper you (lit.) with the advice that you should read the whole work first and only then begin. But I get started right away because I want to hold on to the adventure of it. Yes, the tension has to be kept.]

Ik heb een ontzettende hekel aan om me te vervelen dus ik, eh, ja, ik begin dus bij het begin en dan moet ik vaag veranderen want het blijkt, uit het vervolg blijkt dat ik verkeerd vertaald heb maar ik wil dus die spanning behouden (eh, ja). En, ja dat is mijn enige methode eigenlijk.

[I really detest being bored, so I just start at the beginning and then I very often have to change things because it turns out, later on it emerges that I translated something wrongly but I want to hold on to that tension. And yes that's my only method really.]

Ik zou ja ik zou zeggen "all you need is love" and a good dictionary, natuurlijk (laughs).

[I'd, yes, I'd say "all you need is love," and a good dictionary, of course (laughs).]

There are a number of positions being taken by the translator here in relation not only to his work but also in relation to other (scholarly) discourses on translation. The positions visible in the extract would be understood traditionally as formulations pertaining to an overall translation strategy, but they can also be understood as typifying the various features of genre, for example, which in fact any translation strategy would have to take into account. These positionings are also founded on a couple of key metaphors,[3] metonyms and other forms of figurative speech, that of "cannibalism" being a case in point.

Among some of the other prerequisites of translation set out by the interviewee, we immediately note the following: (a) **"love/fire"**, (b) **"a good dictionary/ finish"**, and (c) **an immediate engagement with the text.**

Lennon and McCartney's "all you need is love," along with a good dictionary, is not only what the translator takes to the text. Taken together, the "love" and the "dictionary" index the creativity and formal care that should become visible in the finished work of translation. The 'fire and the finish', borrowed from the American poet, Robert Lowell,[4] are postulated as (a) being present in the original or source texts, (b) as the modus operandi needed to do justice to those originals, and (c) as traits that should be manifest in the target text or translation. It is interesting to note in this case that the axes of action extend both toward creativity and toward formal care, which on the face of it challenges the commonly held perception that

---

3. For a study of the ideological orientations of metaphor, see Semino 2008

4. This is taken from Lowell's comments on his translations of Puskin's poetry in *Imitations* (1962).

literary translators have and do take more leeway with a text than their colleagues in legal, business or other areas of translation.

Creativity and formal care remain the two tangents of orientation, action and prospective result. It is clear from this extract that 'love' or 'the fire,' though they are easy to associate as metaphors with literary genre, were not merely seen as traits of the work to be translated but also evidenced a disposition combined with a way of working (what has come to be known in the literature as translational habitus), all of which can also be encompassed by more recent definitions of genre, building on Bakhtin (1986), which consider it as a form of action involving language and other semiotic forms in a given cultural space (Bauman in Duranti 2001:79–82).

The most striking metaphor used by the translator is perhaps "cannibalism" or rather "a type of cannibalism." Although I am now unable to verify this due to the translator's untimely death, I doubt that he was referring to the Brazilian movement. However, the works of literature[5] being devoured were mainly written in the English language: devoured in the global language of English, as it were, and regurgitated into Dutch. There was a certain amount of deference noticeable in the utterance and nothing of the political or poetic stance visible in the Brazilian school. In fact, what we have here is a European casting himself as a cannibal, which is something of an about-face. The comparison highlights the translator's acute awareness of the dangers involved in translating works from other languages and cultures but also of the importance of showing the beauty of such works to local audiences (translator as cultural mediator).

Cannibalism, in combination with "see how beautiful" strongly indexes his approach to his translation work. But did he borrow it from the Brazilians or does this discourse in fact describe his own translation practice? It is argued here that possible answers to these questions can be proposed by first examining the metaphor along with the other metaphors and metonyms formulated in the overall narratives and then contrasting them with findings from a corpus analysis of his translations. This would establish a link between actual translation practices and the situated theories informing them that are indexed by these metaphors and metonyms (Flynn 2006).

As was pointed out above, perhaps our search for origins, though useful in establishing the scope of a concept, may obscure the situated understandings and uses of such concepts in the Dutch context. Hence, it would seem that both avenues need to be explored at once in order to gain a clearer understanding of what is going on, i.e., in terms of both translational and discursive practices. One thing is clear, however: the translator's use of the concept had little or no impact on conceptualizations of translation in Flanders and the Netherlands, as is also the case

---

5. These works stemmed from the United States, the Caribbean, Great Britain and Ireland.

for the rich array of concepts used by the other translators in the study, which does not mean that their theorizations are any less valid or worthy of consideration than those found in the literature.

Another stance visible in the extract is a certain reticence with regard to textbook views on translation strategy. Various variations on this stance were elicited from all those who participated in the study. These variations can be placed along a cline ranging from a rejection of Translation Studies and its relevance for translation to a softened form of irony toward, if not pity for, what they view as the obscurantist preoccupations of translation scholars. This first became visible in their initial resistance toward participation in the project: I was an academic after all. And while the translator did quote Lowell's "the fire and the finish," Lowell can hardly be considered a translation scholar.

In general, the arguments made on the basis of the data extract quoted above also hold for the other translators who agreed to participate in the study for their narratives also contained a wealth of such formulations. In order to show that the metaphors found in the extract were indeed not isolated instances, I am including a table here (Table 1) which contains a list of pivotal remarks made by other translators along with their relevance in relation to their perceptions of genre (Bauman in Duranti 2001) and how this impacts on their translations.

As was stated in the Introduction, many other translators operating below the horizon of academic visibility have equally insightful things to say about their practices and hence to share with translation scholars. Hopefully, the data discussed here illustrates the point. As was also stated above, whether their theorizing coincides with their practices needs to be verified by corpus analysis and contrastive study and this also holds for the translations of prominent translators and pivotal metaphors they use and further develop into working models and conceptualizations of translation.[6]

Conclusion

It is suggested here that the insights gleaned from ethnographic studies deserve a place of prominence in the daily business of Translation Studies, namely in the articulation of incisively sharper formulations of our understanding of translation. In returning to the various reconceptualizations of translation found in Gentzler's book, I would also suggest that works on translation such as those written by Suzanne Jill Levine and others could be read, following Mary Louise Pratt (1992),

---

6. For a detailed discussion of this and other key issues regarding well-known poets and translators translating poetry into English, see Robinson 2010

Table 1. Genre-related utterances in the data — a schematic overview

Ref.	Metaphor/ Metonym	English Translation	Form of language use	Accompanying expectations/ evaluations	Framing activity	Focus/Approach
5.1.1 Ext. 3–30	"The fire and the finish" / "love and a good dictionary"		Translating poetry	Respect for the original in every sense	Translation	Creative immediacy and formal care in translation
5.1.2 Ext. 3–31	"Doordringen in een tekst tot op het bot"	"Penetrating to the bone of a text"	Translating poetry	Improvement of one's poetic/ translation practice	Translation	Meaning making through translation
5.1.3 Ext. 3–32	"Van één machinetje een ander machinetje, apparaatje maken"	"Making one machine or apparatus out of another"	Translating poetry	Difference in/across language(s) forms basis for leeway in a genre	Translation	Shifting dynamic functions of poems forms framework of translation
5.1.4 Ext. 3–33	"De adem van de dichter"	"The poet's breath"	Translating poetry	A poet's breath determines his/ her poetry (meter, line)	Translation	Breath as a means of analysis and translation
5.1.5 Ext. 3–34	"Dicht op je huid"	"Close to the skin"	Translating poetry	(Possible disappointment at) a poet's generic shortcomings	Translation	Empathy as a basis for translational action
5.1.6 Ext. 3–35	"Klamme handen"	"Sweaty hands"	Translating poetry/ prose	Anxiety regarding one's poetic/ translational competence	Translation	Orders of generic competence: exclusion from /inclusion in translation practice
5.1.7 Ext. 3–36	"Geen vast recept"	"No fixed recipe"	Translating prose	Eye for individual or changing literary styles	Translation	Engaging with/ identifying differences within known generic frameworks
5.1.8 Ext. 3–37	"Een soort afwijking"	"A kind of aberration"	Translating prose/ poetry	(Preference for) certain historical periods within genres	Translation	Wish to Translate = an aberration Understanding Pre and High Modernism

as auto-ethnographies of translation, building on the assumption that each writer/ translator's work contains his/her own situated theories on translation and the language and cultural repertoires and practices involved. As a corrective to the power and visibility differential involved, I would suggest that the broader ethnographies be read alongside these auto-ethnographies and larger sociologies of translation before any over-arching theories, resistant or otherwise, are posited. In this way translators can be viewed and theorized in their plurality. Visibility as such should also be differentiated, as the data used for this study suggests. For the translators who participated in this study, visibility meant recognition by their colleagues, not being mentioned alongside the authors they translate.

What does become evident from contrasting (the views of) lesser known translators and those who have entered the field of vision of translation scholars is in fact a variation on the power differential (known/unknown; visible/invisible), which may be overshadowed by dominant discourses on continental power in Translation Studies. It would be interesting, therefore, to examine precisely how certain metaphors acquire symbolic power and become productive working models for translation or begin to define approaches to translation in a given cultural space. Does this happen to the detriment of or in competition with other metaphors or models in their immediate purview? It is from this point of inception that scholarly models of description and explanation often emerge, viz. the many reconceptualizations of translation found in recent writing following the "cultural" and the "power turn." It is also the point at which the two strands of argument pursued in this paper meet.

On a related note, one of the paradoxical upshots of championing resistance to Western or Eurocentric translation studies may be that it will silence those who are resisting them by enmeshing them in a hegemonic academic discourse they are purportedly attempting to escape from in trying to find their own voices — the vital paradox of representation that led to Clifford and Marcus's seminal work, *Writing Culture* (Clifford and Marcus 1986).

To conclude, a blanket rejection of former "Western" or "Euro-centric" approaches to translation scholarship might serve another purpose: continually calling for a re-examination of existing theories for re-examination's sake and, in so doing, placing the scholar safely on the "right" side of a political and ideological "goodie-baddie" equation in the struggle for academic credence. Suggestions, proposals, calls and further philosophical speculations on the name and nature of translation should not be used to disguise a *fuite en avant* that allows scholars to dispense with the necessity of examining the consequences or results, on the ground, of the theories they reject and the "radical" new theories they propose.

As Bourdieu pointed out (Bourdieu 2001), the countering of existing (orthodox) theory by radical new theory should not only be understood in terms of the relative superiority or validity of the models being proposed or their greater power to generate deeper insight but also in terms of how scholars position themselves in the academic field and envision and construct their own career trajectories. That any theory, radical or conservative, can be overthrown or found to be lacking is a commonplace. That any theory can uphold a cultural or social situation it was purposely designed to undermine and combat is perhaps a less obvious thought but one we should nonetheless bear in mind.

References

Angelelli, Claudia V. 2004. Medical Interpreting and Cross-cultural Communication. Cambridge: Cambridge University Press.

Appiah, Kwame Anthony. 1993. "Thick Translation." Special issue on "Post-Colonial Discourse" guest-edited by Tejumola Olaniyan. *Callaloo* 16.4 (Fall):808–819.

Bachmann-Medick, Doris. 2006. "Meanings of translation in cultural anthropology" In: Theo Hermans, Translating others 1 pp. 33–42.

Baker, Mona. 2001. 'The Pragmatics of Cross-Cultural Contact and Some False Dichotomies in Translation Studies." In *CTIS Occasional Papers*, Volume 1, edited by Maeve Olohan, 7–20. Manchester: Centre for Translation & Intercultural Studies, UMIST.

Bourdieu, Pierre. 2001. *Science de la Science et Réflexivité*. Paris: Editions Raisons d'Agir.

Canale, M. 1983. "From Communicative Competence to Communicative Language Pedagogy." In *Language and Communication*, edited by J.C. Richards & R. W. Schmidt, 2–27. London & New York: Longman.

Chesterman, Andrew. 1993. "From 'Is' to 'Ought': Translation Laws, Norms and Strategies." *Target* 5.1:1–20.

Cheung, Martha. 2006. *An Anthology of Chinese Discourse on Translation*. Manchester: St. Jerome Publishing.

Cheung, Martha, P. Y. 2007. "On Thick Translation as a Mode of Cultural Representation." In *Across Boundaries: International Perspectives on Translation Studies*, edited by Dorothy Kenny & Kyongjoo Ryou, 22–37. Newcastle upon Tyne: Cambridge Scholars Publishing.

Clifford, James & Marcus, George. 1986. *Writing Culture: the poetics and politics of ethnography*. Berkeley: University of California Press.

Duranti, Alessandro (ed.). *Key Terms in Language and Culture*. Malden: Blackwell.

Flynn, Peter. 2006. *A Linguistic Ethnography of Literary Translation: Irish poems and Dutch-speaking translators*. Ghent University: unpublished doctoral dissertation.

Geertz, Clifford. [1973] 2000. *The Interpretation of Cultures*. New York: Basic Books.

Gentzler, Edwin. 2008. *Translation and Identity in the Americas: New Directions in Trasnlation Theory*. London: Routledge.

Gouanvic, Jean-Marc. 1997. "Pour une sociologie de la traduction : le cas de la littérature américaine traduite en France après la seconde guerre mondiale (1945–1960)." In *Translation as Intercultural Communication*, edited by Mary Snell-Hornby, Zuzana Jettmarová, and Klaus Kaindl, 33–44. Amsterdam: John Benjamins Publishing Company.

Gouanvic, Jean-Marc. 2005. "A Bourdieusian theory of translation, or the coincidence of practical instances: field, 'habitus', capital and 'illusio'" In: Moira Inghilleri, Bourdieu and the sociology of translation and interpreting 11:2. pp. 147–166.

Hermans, Theo. 2003. 'Cross-Cultural Translation Studies as Thick Translation', 380–89. University of London: Bulletin of the School of Oriental and African Studies 66, 3.

Hermans, T. 2006. *Translating Others*. (1, 2). Manchester: St Jerome.

Hymes, Dell. H. 1971. *On Communicative Competence*. Philadelphia: University of Pennsylvania Press.

Inghilleri, Moira. 2005. "Mediating Zones of Uncertainty: Interpreter Agency, the Interpreting Habitus and Political Asylum Adjudication." *The Translator* 11.1:69–85.

Kiberd, Declan.1995. *Inventing Ireland*. London: Vintage.

Koller, Werner. 1976. "Äquivalenz in kontrastiver Linguistik und Übersetzungswissenschaft" in Grähs L., Korlén G. & Malmberg, B. (eds.) *Theory and Practice of Translation*, Nobel Symposium 39, Bern: Lang.

Koskinen, Kaisa. 2008. *Translating Institutions: An Ethnographic Study of EU Translation* Manchester: St. Jerome Publishing.

Levine, Suzanne Jill. 1991. *The Subversive Scribe: Translating Latin American Fiction*. St. Paul: Graywolf Press.

Maryns, Katrijn. 2006. *The asylum speaker. Language in the Belgian asylum procedure*. Manchester: St. Jerome.

Massardier-Kenney, Françoise. 1997. "Towards a Redefinition of Feminist Translation Practice." *The Translator* 3 (1): 55–69.

Pratt, Mary Louise.1992. *Imperial eyes: Travel Writing and Transculturation*. London and New York: Routledge.

Pym, Anthony. 1998. *Method in Translation History*, Manchester: St. Jerome.

Pym, Anthony, Miriam Shlesinger & Zuzana Jettmarová (eds). 2006. *Sociocultural aspects of translating and interpreting*. Amsterdam & Philadelphia: John Benjamins.

Robinson, Douglas. 2002. *Western Translation Theory from Herodotus to Nietzsche*. Manchester: St Jerome Publishing.

Robinson, Peter. 2010. *Poetry & Translation. The Art of the Impossible*. Liverpool: Liverpool University Press.

Sela-Sheffy, Rakefet. 2006. "The Pursuit of Symbolic Capital by a Semi-Professional Group: The Case of Literary Translators in Israel." In *Übersetzen — Translating — Traduire: Towards a "Social Turn"?*, edited by Michaela Wolf, 243–252. Münster-Hamburg-Berlin-Wien-London: LIT.

Semino, Elena. 2008. *Metaphor in Discourse*. Cambridge: Cambridge University Press.

Silverstein, Michael & Greg Urban. 1996. *Natural Histories of Discourse*. Chicago: University of Chicago Press.

Simeoni, Daniel. 1998. "The Pivotal Status of the Translator's Habitus." *Target* 10.1: 1–39.

Snell-Hornby, Mary. 2006. *The turns of translation studies. New paradigms or shifting viewpoints?* Amsterdam & Philadelphia: Benjamins (Benjamins translation library, 66).

Sturge, Kate. 1997. 'Translation Strategies in Ethnography', *The Translator* 3(1): 21–38.

Sturge, Kate. 2007. *Representing Others. Translation, Ethnography and the Museum*. Manchester: St Jerome.

Toury, Gideon. 1995. *Descriptive Translation Studies and Beyond*. Amsterdam/Philadelphia: John Benjamins Publishing Company.

Tymoczko, Maria. 2005. "Reconceptualising Western Translation Theory: Integrating Non-Western Thought about Translation." In *Translating Others*, edited by Theo. Hermans, 13–32. Manchester: St. Jerome Publishing.

Tymoczko, Maria and Edwin Gentzler (eds.). 2002. *Translation and Power.* Amherst: University of Massachusetts Press.

Tymoczko, Maria. 2009. "Why Translators Should Want to Internationalize Translation Studies." *The Translator* 15.2: 401–21.

Venuti, Lawrence (1995) *The Translator's Invisibility, a History of Translation.* London & New York: Routledge.

Venuti, Lawrence (ed.). 2000. *The Translation Studies Reader.* London: Routledge

Wolf, Michaela. 2003. "Feminist thick translation: A challenge to the formation of feminist cultural identity?" *Tradução e Comunicação* 12: 115–131.

Wolf, Michaela and Fukari, Alexandra (eds). 2007. *Constructing a Sociology of Translation.* Amsterdam: John Benjamins.

Beyond "Eurocentrism"?

The challenge of linguistic justice theory to translation studies

Michael Boyden

This paper deals with the recurrent criticism in Translation studies in general and Anglophone Translation studies in particular that the discipline labors under a 'Eurocentric' bias. The author develops two arguments in relation to this. First, the charge of 'Eurocentrism' serves a number ends that have less to do with an actual desire to reach out to 'non-Western' discourses on translation (although the globalization of the discipline has definitely broadened the scope and concerns of translation scholars) than with a generation gap among translation scholars. Drawing on literature from the last two decades, the author argues that 'Eurocentrism' often functions as an asymmetrical counterconcept, in Reinhart Koselleck's sense, which allows translation scholars to legitimize their scholarly project by investing it with a sense of urgency and political relevance. In a second step, the author argues that the rhetorical debate on 'Eurocentrism' often suffers from an overextension of identity claims, whereby translation processes are reduced to either an imposition of or reaction against hegemonic power structures. This focus on identity, however legitimate, may result in linguistic paternalism. To counteract this negative effect, the author calls for a revalorization of instrumentalist justifications of language use by drawing on linguistic justice theory, arguing that, following recent insights by political philosophers and contrary to the prevalent view held by translation scholars, when it comes to determining a just translation policy, (non-linguistic) instrumental concerns tend to override (intrinsic) identity concerns.

Introduction: Understanding the politics of "beyond"

One of the prevailing buzz words in Translation studies during the last couple of decades has been that of 'Eurocentrism.' Open any new publication in the field and it is very likely you will encounter high-flown proclamations warning against the implicit or explicit adoption of models that may be considered 'Eurocentrist.' It may well be that this concept has proven so efficacious because it articulates a generational difference, both within the discipline of Translation studies and in society at large. The globalization of Translation studies as a scholarly enterprise has resulted in a critical engagement with its European roots and presuppositions, especially since the rise of postcolonial and feminist approaches highlighting power relations between dominant and emerging literatures and cultures. In the American context, in particular, the recurring charge of 'Eurocentrism' has served to align the discipline with broader debates within the U.S. over the nation's history and identity which, roughly since the 1950s, have pitched the white 'Euro-American' majority against various minority cultures claiming equal representation. Although there are obvious parallels and linkages between the decolonization movements in developing nations and the struggles of minorities against the 'internal colonization' of the North American continent by descendants of European explorers, it is clear that the meanings of 'Eurocentrism' in these contexts are not entirely coterminous.

This indicates that the notion of 'Eurocentrism' can apply to very diverse, possibly conflicting historical realities. In the following I will argue that most often 'Eurocentrism' functions as an asymmetrical counterconcept, in the sense of Reinhart Koselleck, i.e., a term that serves to "deny the reciprocity of mutual recognition" (Koselleck 2004: 156). As Koselleck has pointed out, groups need concepts to define themselves by setting themselves off from others. They may do so by means of simple oppositions of the type Protestants versus Catholics, or Italians versus Greeks. In order to become politically and socially functional, however, groups tend to make exclusive claims to linguistically universal concepts: The Catholic or Protestant Church becomes *the* Church, meaning that everybody outside that specific religious community is automatically considered a non-believer or even an heretic; or, everyone outside the Greek nation is identified not as a citizen of another nation but as a barbarian. In such cases, we are dealing with global duals (Christian/heathen, Hellene/barbarian) with a clear, built-in preference for one side of the opposition (unless, of course, the opposition is turned against itself, as when a group adopts a disparaging label as a badge of honor, but even in such cases the structural asymmetry persists).

However indispensible, asymmetrical counterconcepts cannot be conflated with the historical or institutional groupings they help to create. As Koselleck suggests, this is already evident from the fact that these concepts, despite their seemingly universalist appeal, change their import over time in accordance with shifting realities: those who were barbarians or heretics before all of a sudden become allies, or vice versa. Elsewhere, I have argued that the discipline of American literary history asserted its autonomy by constantly reacting against earlier self-definitions, thus paradoxically cementing its identity by systematically destabilizing itself on a rhetorical level (Boyden 2009). While the pioneers of American literature studies principally positioned themselves against the assumed subservience to the 'Anglo-Saxon' mother culture by pointing attention to other 'European' (non-English) aspects of American identity, during the latter half of the century that 'European' heritage had itself become suspect because of the reconfiguration of the nation's self-image in response to, among other things, the Civil Rights movement, mass-scale immigration from non-European countries, and U.S. military involvement in South-East Asia and Latin America. Although it is now the 'Euro-American' rather than the 'Anglo-Saxon' power center that is subject to scrutiny, the asymmetrical semantic structure at the basis of these counterconcepts — that which triggers ever new attempts to go beyond established definitions in an attempt to speak to *the* people as a whole (a necessarily impossible undertaking, given the selectivity of literary history as a genre) — has seldom been questioned. Indeed, it is this shared motivational structure at the core of a discipline which at once guarantees and obscures the continuation of the motivational logic that leads us to disqualify the ideas of our predecessors as 'provincial', 'racist', 'sexist', and so on.

By drawing attention to the self-implicatory logic of these counterconcepts, I by no means wish to deny the validity or pertinence of certain critiques of 'Eurocentrism' in Translation studies. The discipline's move away from purely descriptive and functionalist approaches toward broader considerations of the cultural and political implications of translation issues has opened up interesting new vistas for research. Engaging with translation not merely as a means of bringing something across but as an instrument of nation formation and imperialism may have given the discipline a sense of relevance and urgency which it previously did not possess. However, I also see real dangers in this sociopolitical "responsabilization" of Translation studies. The desire to unearth the ideological unconscious of the discipline by showing how traditional models (consciously or not) exclude 'non-Western' voices or perspectives, if it fails to address deeper institutional concerns, may in the end itself get mired in a utopian rhetoric of inclusivity, which may even copy the semantics of nineteenth century nationalism (out of which translation studies can be said to have emerged). What is seldom taken into consideration is that those models that are now criticized for being 'Eurocentric' are themselves a reaction against an institutional matrix that was at some point considered to be exclusionist or reductive. With the globalization of Translation studies, the stakes of the debate have of course shifted dramatically, but as I hope to show the inner logic of the discipline is pretty much intact. Translation scholars continue to define themselves (which means: to exclude and to select) by going 'beyond' earlier methods and ideas, by drawing boundaries through the application of linguistically universal concepts to specific social realities.

This article consists of two parts. Firstly, I review how a number of translation scholars, particularly in the American context, have availed themselves of the concept of 'Eurocentrism' to carve out a place for themselves in the discipline and to differentiate their views on translation from established approaches. I argue that, in doing so, they tend to draw on a utopian semantics of inclusiveness, which may result in linguistic paternalism. Secondly, I show how Translation studies can benefit from insights from linguistic justice theory as a corrective to overdrawn ideological claims connected to the rhetoric of inclusiveness.

The uses of 'Eurocentrism' in translation studies

In their introduction to *The Metalanguage of Translation*, a 2009 republication of a 2007 special issue of *Target*, Yves Gambier and Luc van Doorslaer argue that "time has come to challenge the so-called Eurocentric bias of Translation studies by exploring the diversity of 'non-Western' discourses on and practices of translation, if only to illustrate that metadiscussion is one of the most complex, unrewarding, perhaps undisciplined topics in the discipline" (2009: 1). The conditional clause at the end of this quote is revealing, insofar as it suggests how the metadiscussion on the ideological presuppositions of Translation studies is emotionally loaded. The quote reveals that the insistent call for broadening the scope of the discipline to include 'non-Western' perspectives is about more than merely extending our available knowledge about translation and its role in society. Going beyond 'Eurocentrism' is as much about 'setting things straight' as it is about 'getting things right', i.e., showing how for centuries translation has functioned as an instrument for the 'West' to subdue or conquer the 'Rest' (that the borders between what counts as the 'West' and what falls out of it have shifted dramatically over time seems evident but is often conveniently shoved under the carpet by those applying these labels). As Theo Hermans notes in a recent article on the ethical, cultural and political turns in Translation Studies, the feminist and postcolonialist critiques of traditional translation theory are above all about 'reparation' (2009: 100). These approaches have more to do with 'intervening' than with 'describing', insofar as they are set on counteracting the harm done by male-dominated, Western society and reconstructing our (supposedly 'descriptive') theories of the world on the basis of more egalitarian conceptions of sex, gender and race. My aim here is to understand the institutional logic behind this generalized reaction against the 'Eurocentrist' roots of Translation studies.

It bears remarking that the collective interest in 'non-Western' discourses on translation, although strongly inspired by scholars and thinkers with roots elsewhere (such as Edward Said, Frantz Fanon, Gayatri Spivak, Homi Bhabha, and others), for the most part emerged in the intellectual centers of what is called 'the West'. In the United States, in particular, growing awareness of 'non-Western' viewpoints can be framed in relation to the rise of cultural studies, which was shaped by scholars who came of age during the Civil Rights era. As the historian Matthew Jacobson has pointedly noted, the rise of the roots phenomenon in the United States and the emergence of the 'politics of white grievance' has to be interpreted as a consequence of the sharpening of the color line since the 1950s and 1960s (2006: 35). Whites who before had been relatively comfortable in the Anglo mainstream were now eager to stress how they too had been victimized by a society that denied the ethnic and linguistic diversity of its population. In my opinion, the strong investment in identity issues which has characterized Translation Studies since the 1980s and 1990s can at least in part be explained in terms of this ethnic revival in U.S. culture, where 'Eurocentrism' refers above all to the dominant position of people of European origin as opposed to 'people of color' (such as blacks, Latinos, and Asian Americans). The point is an important one, because it shows how the turn towards 'non-Western' perspectives stem from what was essentially *domestic* unease about the ethnolinguistic make-up of the U.S. In such a fraught context, it is a matter of no small debate what it means to be 'European' or to claim a 'European' heritage. But when, as has happened in Translation Studies, debates about 'Eurocentrism' are extended to other constellations as well, other concerns are added to the mix and things get even more complex.

Consider the following examples. In his oft-quoted contribution to Lawrence Venuti's collection *Rethinking Translation*, the translator of Egyptian literature Richard Jacquemond argues provocatively that "because translation theory (as well as literary theory in general) has developed on the almost exclusive basis of the European linguistic and cultural experience, it relies on the implicit postulate of an egalitarian relationship between different linguistic and cultural areas" (1992: 140). Jacquemond's claim makes sense in relation to the dilemmas faced by Egyptian writers growing up in a hybrid culture shaped by French colonial institutions and local Arabic traditions. As Jacquemond himself notes, the opposition between Europe and the Third World should in this case be understood as an opposition between North and South, and more specifically between France and Egypt (and not, for example, the Maghrib countries, were the situation is markedly different). Still, Jacquemond links this case to a broader "political economy" of translation, based on a typically "Western discourse" of linguistic equality or equivalence. The tenet of equivalence has of course become a preferred target of translation theory. It was widely questioned even before the rise of postcolonial studies, and by scholars working within a framework now deemed 'Eurocentric'. But the postcolonial paradigm has increased the relevance of this critique insofar as it explicitly links the illusion of linguistic equality to issues of social and political inequality. By generalizing from the Egyptian case (even while indicating differences within the Arab world and among hegemonic powers), Jacquemond manages to explain the cultural "schizophrenia" of the Third World in terms of the lingering influence of the "European linguistic and cultural experience" on translation exchanges and theories. This adds force to his argument but also serves to gloss over linguistic power struggles among 'Western' nations.

A similar dynamic seems to be at work in the 2000 volume *Beyond the Western Tradition* edited by Marilyn Gaddis Rose. I focus in particular on the contribution by Joshua Price entitled "Hybrid Languages, Translation, and Post-Colonial Challenges." Price takes issue with "mainstream translation theory" (Nida, Lefevere, Toury, Bassnett, even Venuti), which according to him is based on "an ideology or even a cosmological ordering which is part of the constitution of the identity of the West or Occident" (27). Drawing on the work of feminists (Massey) and postcolonial thinkers (Coronil, Fanon, Memmi, Dussel, Niranjana), as well as Walter Benjamin (who seems to be everybody's best friend), Price argues that the assumption of a strict dichotomy between source and target languages is rooted in a "Eurocentric perspective," which clashes with the reality of linguistic hybridity (30). Exactly what Price means by this "Eurocentric perspective" remains unclear however. It is associated variously with "the influence of structuralist linguistics" (25); with "the widespread tendency in the U.S. and Western Europe to deny the ways in which different cultures and languages interact with each other" (32); or with "neo-colonialist fantasies of purity" (42). Yet, judging from the examples which Price uses to back up his claims (James Baldwin, Pat Mora, Guillermo Gómez-Peña), he seems to be taking aim mostly at the Euro-American majority in the U.S. (excluding ethnic minorities like Jewish Americans, to which Price himself belongs) which would not be open to the kind of double entendres and linguistic border crossing which animates minority writing. Covering all these conflicting realities, Eurocentrism here above all functions as a useful counterconcept to mark the ascendancy of a new generation of translation scholars as well as to justify new entries in the pantheon of American letters.

Maria Tymoczko is prominent among those scholars in the discipline who have called for a reorientation of its theoretical presuppositions. In a 2006 article entitled "Reconceptualizing Translation Theory," building on ideas developed in earlier publications (a.o. Tymoczko 1999) she points out some of the flaws of what she labels the "positivist" tradition in translation research, a tradition that is in her opinion dominated by "Western" or "Eurocentric" theories and models. The pernicious effects of this problematic but apparently persistent tradition, which Tymoczko does not demarcate in great detail apart from a few references to the godfathers of the discipline (such as Cicero, Schleiermacher, and Matthew Arnold), would be apparent, among other things, in translation scholars' overemphasis on the written word, their restrictive focus on canonical texts and text types, the normalization of monolingualism (and, consequently, the marginalization of hybrid, plurilingual cultural situations), and the exclusive identification of translation as interlingual mediation or communication. As an alternative to these flawed conceptions, Tymoczko puts forward a "postpositivist" framework which, as she suggests, will open up the discipline to "non-Western" approaches and data by redefining translation in terms of the notions of transference (which frames linguistic transfers in relation to other forms of transmission), representation (highlighting the constructivist aspect of translation), and transculturation (conceptualizing translation as one means, among others, to perform identities), respectively.

Rather than targeting specific translation theories, Tymoczko uses labels such as "Western" and "European" as encompassing counterconcepts in order to identify persistent stereotypes of translation. Occasionally, however, she considerably narrows things down, as when she ascribes the tendency to reduce translation to communication between distinct, monolingual groups to a specifically "Anglo-American model of linguistic (in)competence," a turn that she explains by suggesting that Translation studies "has, after all, been heavily theorized by English speakers, who are notoriously deficient in language acquisition, and who, thus, may be particularly biased in their theorizing of translation" (16, 17).[1] In other words, Tymoczko here justifies her project of reconfiguring translation theory by drawing attention to the perceived monolingualism of the dominant English-speaking nations. This argument strikes me as weak, given Tymoczko's insistence that Translation studies should overcome its historical limitations. This, in my opinion, is precisely what Tymoczko here fails to do, as she rather facilely mixes together the Greco-Roman tradition with what appears to be the global ascendancy of the American nation during the latter half of the twentieth century. Moreover, it is unclear to me how she can square her call to go "beyond professionalism" and "Western" conceptions of translational competence with claims about English speakers being "notoriously deficient in language acquisition." If, as Tymoczko claims, there are a lot of translation exchanges going on within supposedly monolingual communities (oral and written), which heretofore have insufficiently been studied by translation scholars, it is unclear why this finding cannot be extended to Anglo-American society as well, even if it is culturally hegemonic. In her attempt

---

1. At another point in her article, Tymoczko attributes the "Eurocentric" conception of translation to the Latin root of the word, and the kind of meanings that it evokes. As she puts it, "it may be the linguistic implications of the words for translation in [English and Romance languages] that are partly responsible for the tendency of Western translation theory to become embroiled in fruitless arguments about the nature of translation equivalence" (2006: 23).

to open up Translation studies to presentist concerns (presentist in the sense of addressing current identity needs of specific minority groups), Tymoczko's claims about the imperialist presuppositions of European translation theory to some extent serve to reify categories and distinctions that are in reality highly volatile and historically specific.

As a final example of the ways in which 'Eurocentrism' has been put to use in translation theory, I would like to consider Edwin Gentzler's *Translation and Identity in the Americas* (2008). Drawing on new developments in both translation theory and area studies, Gentzler draws attention to a body of scholarship that highlights the important role played by mistranslations, domesticating translations, as well as non-translation in the perpetuation of power structures in both North and South America. Gentzler declares his allegiance to the Manipulation School in Translation Studies, and in particular to the target-oriented approach propagated by Gideon Toury and others, who stress the relativity of definitions of translation. But Gentzler also proposes to go *beyond* Toury by considering not just what at a given moment and place is defined as a translation inside a specific target culture, but also "translation phenomena that occur but may not be defined as such" (2). In this way, Gentzler focuses on practices that are not normally registered by an officially sanctioned culture but are no less important for the identity formation of specific minority groups, which often remain excluded from membership in dominant institutions. Referring to the writings of Derrida, Spivak, Toni Morrison, and the psychoanalyst Jean Laplanche, Gentzler shows how various cultural groupings in the Americas have used translation — understood not merely as a linguistic transfer but as any kind of expression which reveals traces of "Otherness" in dominant discourses — as "one of the primary tools in their search for their own voice and identity" (179).

This strong focus on identity formation and sociocultural representation leads Gentzler, in a discussion of Eric Cheyfitz's 1997 book *The Poetics of Imperialism*, to question the "Eurocentric assumption" that it would be in the interest of minorities in the U.S. (Native Americans, blacks, immigrants) to "seamlessly translate themselves into the Anglo-American culture" (185). By associating "Eurocentrism" with the pressure to assimilate into or conform to mainstream American culture, Gentzler here demonstrates how more or less implicit translation policies have played an often unacknowledged role in constructing American culture but by marginalizing viewpoints that do not readily fit into the dominant self-image of the nation. The appeal of Gentzler's approach derives in a large part from the fact that he urges the reader to consider the ways in which translation theories, far from being neutral, are deeply implicated in power politics, affecting the daily lives of people in the western hemisphere. Even while stressing that cultures are inherently multiple and hybrid, Gentzler underscores minority groups' unbreakable relation to their mother tongue. It is somewhat ironic, therefore, that in his desire to let minorities in the Americas speak "their own language" (12), Gentzler at the same time to some degree essentializes these hybrid subcultures, approaching them as victims of a monolithic and apparently unchanging hegemonic Anglo-American culture, which systematically enforces "Eurocentric" values.[2]

However selective my overview of the uses of the concept of 'Eurocentrism' in translation theory, it is possible to observe some patterns. In all the above cases, the concept is operationalized as an asymmetric counterconcept in Koselleck's sense, i.e., it is presented as the negative pole of an opposition that is unequally antithetical insofar as nobody would readily embrace the label while everybody likes to warn against its dangerous pervasiveness. The positive side of the dual, on the other hand, appears to be extremely variable — while Jacquemond discusses the cultural resistance of Egyptian writers and translators, Price focuses on ethnic subcultures in the U.S., Tymoczko deals mostly with Irish literature in a postcolonial context, and Gentzler traces continuities between translation practices on both American continents. No doubt, this variability explains the remarkable frequency of the concept of 'Eurocentrism' in recent Translation studies literature. But what exactly does it stand for? All the above examples clearly reject a conception of translation as an equivalent transfer between discrete languages across officially recognized state borders. In reaction to this view, which is constructed as the dominant, mainstream perspective on translation, all four scholars stress the intimate connection between translation and identity. Although it would be hard nowadays to find a translation scholar who entirely denies this connection, it is remarkable how the scholars under discussion insist on it with almost missionary

---

2. In my view, there are both epistemological and ethical problems with Gentzler's position. The epistemological obstacles are evident in Gentzler's adoption of Toury's functionalist approach to translation in combination with a normative commitment to promoting the cause of suppressed identities. Even while indicating that "any accurate description" (6) of the Americas is impossible (as would already be apparent from the inadequacy of the name 'America' itself), Gentzler at the same time indicates that it is the scholar's task to point out the role of "misnamings" in the formation of American identities. The question is whether such a position is logically tenable (while naming a continent after a *conquistador* is by no means innocent, the alternatives may be equally problematic). But there are also difficult ethical implications attached to Gentzler's position. As Gentzler states, the U.S. could have been a more open or democratic society if only it had developed a better translation policy or had been more conscious of its own submerged translation history. This blatant ignorance of the multilingual heritage of the U.S., he argues, comes "at certain costs to the psychic well-being of the nation" (11). Even while stating that the next turn in translation studies "should be a social-psychological one," expanding on and going beyond existing functional approaches (180), Gentzler fails to specify how he intends to measure the psychological effects of linguistic assimilation and why it should necessarily be traumatizing.

zeal. This brings us to a final commonality. To a greater or lesser degree, all four approaches are reparatory in scope, in the sense referred to above by Theo Hermans. Their aim is not just to describe reality but also to show how descriptions of reality are always to some degree implicated in linguistic power struggles, and therefore ideologically suspect. Part of the task of the translation scholar, from this perspective, is to grant agency to dominated cultures by laying bare the workings of the hegemonic 'Western' ideology which continues to oppress cultural minorities struggling for representation.

Toward a revaluation of the instrumental nature of translation

While the recurrent charges of 'Eurocentrism' (of which many more examples could be included) spring from a legitimate concern with ethical and political reparation, they also have a problematic side. Let me clarify my point by drawing on the example, discussed in Tymoczko, of Hawaiian nationalists insisting on translations of government documents into Hawaiian in spite of the fact that for most of them English is their *de facto* mother tongue. For Tymoczko, this case shows that translation is about more than just communication across states and instead reveals the complex identity functions it serves in hybrid cultures, which often cannot draw on established literary traditions for their legitimation, as would be the case in 'Western' nations with a pronounced one-on-one relationship between language and territory. The Hawaiian example, however, may also sensitize us to the limitations of overly identity-based arguments. One can easily imagine a scenario in which the need to cultivate one's ancestral language clashes with more prosaic concerns, such as efficiency and access to the dominant culture. In such cases, translation policies will involve difficult trade-offs between the communicative and symbolic needs of the population, and it is likely that the majority of the Hawaiians would not follow the nationalists if this would deprive them of commercial, educational or other opportunities, in this case associated with the English language. This is a question which Tymoczko does not address, and a similar weakness seems to characterize the views of the other scholars discussed above. All seem to favor an interventionist agenda, but the normative underpinnings of their positions remain vague. Most of the time, the argument revolves around the opposition between translation as communication or as power (with an outspoken preference for the latter option), which in the end proves rather unproductive since few would hold, except for rhetorical reasons, that translation is just about one or the other. The more difficult question is what makes the scales tip over in concrete language planning situations. Should Hawaiians (and other minorities) of necessity learn 'their' native language even if it comes at a considerable social cost (perhaps even denying them certain rights)? How far should we go in stressing the importance of identity?

Very few translation scholars, in their persistent embrace of identity politics, seem to be ready to confront this issue head on. As a consequence, the motivation to 'set things straight' may appear somewhat utopian, even paternalistic. By attaching so much importance to the performative dimension of languages, engaged translation scholars risk reproducing the kind of linguistic imperialism they attribute to 'Western' translation theory. For this reason, I want to again highlight the value of instrumentalist justifications of language use and translation. By instrumentalist, I mean the view that, when it comes to questions of translation and justice, the fulfillment of non-linguistic ends tends to take precedence over other constitutive justifications — which, as will become clear, is not to say that languages are not intrinsically valuable but rather that normative arguments appealing to intrinsic values should take into account other communicative needs (for a more detailed account, see Boyden & De Schutter 2008). While it cannot be denied that, in its early phase, Translation Studies was overly focused on translation as a means of communication *across* cultural groups, thus ignoring the plurilingual dynamic *within* many of those groups, I claim that the pendulum may now have swung too far in the direction of the constitutive dimensions of language and translation. While it cannot be stressed too much that translation plays a crucial role in constructing and demarcating identities, pushing the identity argument too far may result in locking minority groups into assigned slots and thereby restricting their access to dominant societal cultures. I would like to articulate my plea for a return to a more communication-oriented approach to translation by suggesting a dialogue with the emergent field of language rights in political philosophy. Despite its interdisciplinary nature, Translation Studies has to date for the most part bypassed what political theorists have had to say about language issues. This apparent neglect — which, I hasten to add, is mutual — may have to do with the normative slant of the linguistic justice debate. Most of the time, these political theories are designed to change or implement language planning strategies in specific contexts and for this reason have seemingly little to offer to the more hermeneutically inclined scholar. As I want to argue, however, the normativity of the linguistic justice debate not only creates obstacles for Translation Studies but opportunities as well.

On initial reflection, political philosophy seems to have little to contribute to debates about translation and minority writing. If political philosophers discuss translation issues at all, they seem to labor under rather static and surprisingly unempirical conceptions about language in society, which most translation scholars would undoubtedly brand 'Eurocentric'. Even those linguistic justice theorists who strongly insist on minority rights still tend to regard states as discrete monolingual entities, inhabited for the most part by monolingual individuals. What those theories can do, however, is to alert translation scholars to the dangers involved in the identity argument. Most if not all linguistic justice theorists recognize the importance of language in the construction of identity — one notable exception, perhaps, is Brian Barry, who treats languages purely as conventional constructs without any intrinsic significance (Barry 2001). Most of Barry's colleagues, however, do recognize that languages are an important component of who we are and that, therefore, those languages deserve to be protected. Importantly, however, the recognition of the identity value of language does not necessarily lead these scholars to discard instrumentalist claims. On the contrary, in the case of a conflict between constitutive and instrumentalist arguments, as in the case of Hawaiians having to choose between loyalty to their native language (which constitutes their identity) and the benefits involved in speaking English (which brings them social, economic, and political benefits), a number of linguistic justice theorists, among them Daniel Weinstock and Thomas Pogge, have argued that the communicative advantages tend to override the identity concerns as a legitimate basis for language policies.

Daniel K. Weinstock is prominent among those who have drawn attention to the problems involved in the constitutive view on language planning. As he argues, in linguistically homogeneous states a language's potential for anchoring people's identities tends to overlap with its other, communicative functions. The smaller the language group becomes, however, the greater the costs involved in realizing nonlinguistic goals, such as the free expression of one's opinion. The constitutive approach thus often involves difficult trade-offs, and, as Weinstock stresses, in the end the non-identity-related functions of language tend to predominate. For this reason, Weinstock pleads for a version of instrumentalism that does not deny people's strong attachment to their native language for the assertion of their personal or group identity, but which at the same time does not simplistically negate the relevance of instrumentalist justifications for the formulation of language rights — we may extend this to translation rights. Once we comprehend instrumentalism in this way, the debate no longer centers on whether language and translation are primarily about communication or identity; rather, attention shifts away from the functions of language to the normative positions through which these functions are best expressed or maintained. Here the conclusion seems to be that legitimating language rights on the basis of nonlinguistic ends is the safer bet because it avoids the problem of linguistic paternalism. As Weinstock puts it, in their efforts to stress the importance of language for individual identity and nation-building, many scholars

> ... have tended to neglect what would seem to be the most obvious and fundamental aspect of language, namely, its instrumental nature, the fact that it allows

us to communicate, and that, all things equal, we have an interest in communicating as broadly as possible. (Weinstock 2003: 269)

Thomas Pogge defends the instrumentalist case on similar grounds. Discussing the accommodation (minority) rights of Hispanics in the U.S., Pogge takes his cue from Will Kymlicka's oft-quoted claim that, while a state can be neutral in other respects, it cannot be so in relation to language. Because they have to make laws *in* a particular language, legislators will always, wittingly or not, promote specific cultural identities to the exclusion of others (Kymlicka 1995). Contrary to Kymlicka, however, Pogge does not infer from this that a state should at all costs protect minority cultures, even against the (non-linguistic) interests of its members, for instance by sending children from a Hispanic background to public schools where instruction is entirely in Spanish.[3] Such accommodation measures, Pogge indicates, would definitely be beneficial for the survival of Spanish as a native language in a nation dominated by English, but they would at the same time deprive Hispanics of other rights, such as literacy in the country's dominant language as their main gateway to the majority culture. As Pogge phrases it:

> ... my rather cautious stance is motivated by a concern for the moral costs of accommodation rights. Moral costs we should be mindful of include, in particular, 'liberal' costs in terms of freedom and equality, which arise when individuals are used to promote some group interest. (Pogge 2003: 121–2)

Allow me to briefly compare the above claim to one made by Edwin Gentzler in *Translation and Identity in the Americas*, where he discusses "the costs of ... language and cultural assimilation" for minorities in the U.S. (among them Latinos):

> In the Americas, both North and South, language rights are consistently denied in many realms of social and political life — at the hospitals, schools, businesses, voting booths, banks, and social services — invariably in contradiction to the very definitions of equality and liberty that define citizenship. (Gentzler 2008: 183)

Although he fails to specify alternatives for the established, monolingual policies in the Americas, Gentzler's word choice ("consistently," "invariably") suggests that in his opinion these policies are fundamentally unjust and should therefore be replaced by ones that protect the language rights of minority cultures. However, as my brief sketch of Weinstock and Pogge's positions makes clear, state protection of minority languages may in its turn clash with the principles of equality and liberty, especially if anchoring a group's identity in a language (and in one language only) constrains participation in the majority culture. The smaller an ethnolinguistic

---

3. As Pogge notes, it is unclear whether Kymlicka himself would entirely support such a view (Pogge 2003: 118 n.19).

community, the higher the costs involved in defending the linguistic rights of that community against the individual's right to participate in societal culture. In my opinion, these moral costs, which expose the ethical limits of identity-based accounts of linguistic rights, need to be factored into an analysis of translation as a means of empowerment and disempowerment. By doing so, translation scholars may avoid getting tangled up in utopian claims about equality and liberty, which indirectly serve to reinforce rather than replace 'Eurocentric' presuppositions about translation.

References

Barry, Brian. 2001. *Culture and Equality*. Cambridge, MA: Harvard University Press.

Boyden, Michael. 2009. *Predicting the Past: The Paradoxes of American Literary History*. Leuven: Leuven University Press.

Cheyfitz, Eric. 1997. *The Poetics of Imperialism: Translation and Colonization from* The Tempest *to* Tarzan. Philadelphia: University of Philadelphia Press.

De Schutter, Helder and Michael Boyden. 2008. "The Ethics of Language Planning." *ADFL Bulletin* 39.2/3: 7–18.

Fishkin, Shelley Fisher. 2005. "Crossroads of Cultures: The Transnational Turn in American Studies." *American Quarterly* 57.1:17–57.

Gambier, Yves and Luc van Doorslaer. 2009. "How about Meta? An Introduction." In *The Metalanguage of Translation*, edited by Yves Gambier and Luc van Doorslaer, 1–7. Amsterdam/Philadelphia: John Benjamins.

Gentzler, Edwin. 2008. *Translation and Identity in the Americas: New Directions in Translation Theory*. London/New York: Routledge.

Jacobson, Matthew Frye. 2006. *Roots Too. White Ethnic Revival in Post-Civil Rights America*. Cambridge, MA: Harvard University Press.

Jacquemond, Richard. 1992. "Translation and Cultural Hegemony: The Case of French-Arabic Translation." In *Rethinking Translation: Discourse, Subjectivity, Ideology*, edited by Lawrence Venuti, 139–158. London/New York: Routledge.

Koselleck, Reinhart. 2004 [1979]. *Futures Past: On the Semantics of Historical Time*. Keith Tribe (trans., introd.). New York: Columbia University Press.

Kymlicka, Will. 1995. *Multicultural Citizenship*. Oxford: Oxford University Press.

Pogge, Thomas W. 2003. "Accommodation Rights for Hispanics in the United States." In *Language Rights and Political Theory*, edited by Will Kymlicka and Alan Patten, 105–123. Oxford, UK: Oxford University Press.

Porter, Catherine. 2010. "Presidential Address 2009: English Is Not Enough." *Publications of the Modern Language Association of America* 125.3:546–555.

Price, Joshua. 2000. "Hybrid Languages, Translation, and Post-Colonial Challenges." In *Beyond the Western Tradition*. Translation Perspectives XI, edited by Marilyn Gaddis Rose, 23–52. Binghampton, NY: State University of New York.

Tymoczko, Maria. 1999. *Translation in a Postcolonial Context: Early Irish Literature in English Translation*. Manchester: St. Jerome.

——— . 2006. "Reconceptualizing Translation Theory: Integrating Non-Western Thought about Translation." In *Translating Others* Vol. II., edited by Theo Hermans, 13–32. Manchester, UK/Kinderhook, US: St. Jerome.

Weinstock, Daniel. 2003. "The Antimony of Language Policy." In *Language Rights and Political Theory,* edited by Will Kymlicka and Alan Patten, 250–270. Oxford, UK: Oxford University Press.

The representation of agents of translation in (South) Africa

Encountering Gentzler and Madonella

Kobus Marais

This article discusses agency in translation as conceptualized in recent developments in Translation Studies. As a subtext, it poses the representation of its own data as a methodological problem. The article discusses Donald Strachan as a possible agent of translation, probing the implications of his interpreting and translation work in a border setting in South Africa in the late 1800s. It then juxtaposes this perspective with the translation theory of Edwin Gentzler, who claims that translators are creating cultures by way of their work. From this encounter, the author suggests a number of implications for researching translation in Africa. The paper ends by reflecting on its own subtext.

Introducing the encounter

In one of the most topical current debates in Translation Studies, the power of the cultural agent — in this case a translator — is being scrutinized from a variety of perspectives. As a working definition of agency, I refer to Maria Tymoczko (2007: 200–216) who conceptualizes translator agency in the translator's power to change societies by means of their translation choices, i.e., both what and how they translate. Encountering and representing the Other through translation and using this encounter and its representation for particular ideological ends have become a theme of central interest in Translation Studies (see for instance Baker 2006; Hermans 2007; Milton & Bandia 2009; Sturge 2007; Tymoczko 2007).[1] Both Kate Sturge (2007) and Tymoczko (2007) made a forceful argument in favour of multiple perspectives and multiple voices, i.e., complexity, to be acknowledged in situations where the Other is encountered — which typically involves a disproportionate distribution of power.

---

1. I use encounter here in the sense suggested by Assman (1996: 98–100).

Methodologically, I wish to frame this article on agency in translation as a case study in encountering and representing translators as agents. I shall represent Gentzler and Madonella as two perspectives, as two case studies on agency in translation, referring specifically to their implications for the African context.[2] I shall also present their ideas as an encounter between two "Others," looking for strands of meaning in their ideas and work, and in this encounter between them. In this way, I hope to construct a text with multiple voices, including my own, and to use juxtaposition as the mode of logic relating these voices to one another. I frame Madonella and his life as a case study for testing the theories on agency in translation. I frame Gentzler as a representative of the theoretical view that translation creates identity, i.e., that a translator is an agent of cultural formation. For this frame, I refer in particular to his latest work (Gentzler 2008), which obviously builds on earlier work.

By framing the article as a conceptualization in encounters and representations, I am taking both a theoretical and meta-theoretical perspective. I am exploring Gentzler's theory in a different context, but I am also exploring meta-theoretical issues, such as the representation of the Other, using causality to explain relationships in translation, and the complexity of the reality which influences translation decisions. I represent the field of Translation Studies as an encounter of minds, perspectives, histories, cultures, and identities. As a field of study, it is itself a border, a space in which thoughts, methods, and perspectives from different disciplines and approaches encounter one another to create new hybrid forms

---

2. Throughout this paper, I am using notions such as Africa, Western, and local not in essential terms, but as part of the larger discourse on the internationalisation of Translation Studies currently being led Maria Tymoczko and others. These concepts are to a large extent polemical, constructed in opposition to other concepts that have currency in the field of Translation Studies and that are equally constructed. Thinking along the lines suggested by scholars such as Tymoczko and Gentzler, to my mind, implies somewhat of a polemical stance, at least for now. In the development of ideas or ideals, one sometimes has to give polemical names to phenomena which are not in themselves necessarily polemical. For instance, when talking about 'indigenous' knowledge, one calls it such not because it is inherently different from other forms of knowledge, but because, in the dialogue in which you are engaged, you have to set things off against other things. In my reading, the current debate on the internationalisation of Translation Studies calls for an interim phase of polemical thinking, until the field of study has been 'normalised.' Already my representation of Africa calls for a deconstruction of Africa as a singular, stable perspective (e.g., Hountondji 1996: 33–70). As in all of my other work, I intend Africa to be a discursive construct to enable me to posit some kind of encounter between what is conceptualized — but also questioned — as the West, the Americas, and Africa. Gentzler (2008) called his book *Translation and identity in the Americas*, where the Americas are as much a construct as is Africa. Using working concepts thus seems to be an acceptable device in current debates in Translation Studies.

of thoughts, methods, and perspectives. This article is thus itself a border space, a hybrid, just as I, the author, am biologically, ethnically, culturally, linguistically a hybrid — a product of encounters of various natures in border spaces.

Encountering Madonella

Donald Strachan was born in Scotland in 1840 and migrated to the then Natal colony in the south-east of Africa with his family in 1850. He and his older brother, Thomas, were left orphans soon afterward when their mother died in 1851 and their father in 1852. While working for a Durban businessman, the two teenage brothers befriended, among others, Sayimani Rhadebe, with whom they resided for a while, and who played a role in introducing them to the hinterland and its peoples. Their work as transport riders took them into parts of the colony where they made contact with groups of indigenous people and picked up various languages and dialects. In the process, they also picked up business skills and a feel for the politics of the land. In 1858, they settled on the Umzimkulu River where they opened a store.[3] Through the next half century, Donald Strachan lived in this area and involved himself in business, politics, law, farming, and the military — as well as interpreting. It was through his acceptance in indigenous communities that his name Donald was translated into a Bantu form "Madonella".[4] This translation or re-christening was indicative of a change of identity — at least from the side of the people who gave it to him. The British would never call him Madonella — for them, he was Strachan or Donald or Donald Strachan. These names indicate different identities associated with two worlds that would seldom meet. Madonella died in 1915, leaving behind a business empire that lasted well into the twentieth century (Snell 2005).

My aim is not a representation of the details of his life, which has been documented in a number of sources, nor is it a comprehensive overview of his life or the implications thereof.[5] Rather, I wish to present a number of representations of him which may shed light on the complex role of agents in translation, and on their role in representing the Other. What I hope to demonstrate is that the encounter with Madonella I offer the reader is a constructed representation, which may have

---

3. About a 100 kms northwest of Durban.

4. The name is pronounced with the emphasis on the "o".

5. I here follow Pym's (1998: 20–84) advice to, initially, only unearth as much data as is needed for the current argument. This does not mean that much more about Madonella's original writings and other primary documentation from the era would not yield more perspectives.

very little to do with his intentions in life and much with mine. I am using the history of Madonella to argue a theoretical point concerning agency in contemporary Translation Studies. The way in which I present my argument, I hope, will introduce notions regarding the complexity of representation into the metadiscourse of Translation Studies. I am exploring the ways in which Madonella, as what would today be called a community interpreter, contributed to the creation of a particular identity in the community in which he lived. My interest is in not only his own identity as a translator/interpreter but also in the identity, that is, the sense of self-definition or self-image, that his work has created in the Kokstad community. What was his role/identity? Interpreter, politician, magistrate, businessman, warrior, human being, Scot, Natalian, colonist, indigenous leader? What kind of identity did he create by means of his interpreting? What I want to argue is that Madonella does not speak for himself and neither does he speak with one voice. Also, I am assuming that his legacy cannot be construed coherently — that many forces played him and that he played with many forces.

Let me start by suggesting that the geopolitical area into which Madonella entered was a factor in creating his identity. What is currently known as the Kokstad area or Griqua-land East (in the west of what is now the province of KwaZulu-Natal in South Africa) was known as Nomansland in the days of Madonella. As both Margaret Rainier (2002) and Milner Snell (2005) explain, it was called so not because nobody lived there, but because it was under nobody's control. It was a sparsely populated area inhabited by various tribal groups or even individuals, and it fell under the rule of neither Natal nor the Cape Colony. Furthermore, neither Isizulu- nor isiXhosa- nor Sesotho-speaking groups were in control of the area or claimed it. Into this seeming political void stepped Madonella, who was soon acknowledged as a language mediator by most of the indigenous groups, later on by the Griqua,[6] and, at times, by the British colonial rulers.[7] Was it a matter of the situation creating the man or the man creating the situation? Referring to Andrew Chesterman's (2000; 2008) notions of causality, what will it take to prove that the geopolitical context into which Madonella stepped was a condition for translation, i.e., a cause? Would he have been the force he was if he had lived in another space? Would he still have had the enormous influence ascribed to him if he had stepped into a well-organized society? It seems as though the particular context played at least some role in facilitating the use of his language acumen to political effect.

---

6. The Griqua is a Southern African group of people of mixed decent. Among their ancesters count mostly Khoi people mixed with white settlers, San, and other groups.

7. See for instance Balson's (2007) work on the larger history of the Qriqua, an indigenous group of people in South Africa.

Soon after Madonella had settled in Nomansland, the Griqua under Adam Kok III also settled there (see Balson 2007, Rainier 2002, Snell 2000, 2005). They immediately forged a good relationship, and Madonella was appointed by the Griqua, who managed the area on behalf of the British, to take charge of tribal affairs. In exchange, he received farms and business rights from the Griqua. In this regard, Snell (2005) paints Madonella as quite a complex person, who not only had shrewd political insight, but who also benefited financially from his political acumen. The Griqua used his knowledge of local tribes and languages to mediate and to settle political matters in their territory. Would one be correct in arguing that his good connections with the Griqua provided him with the context to have an influence and to be an agent of a particular kind? Seeing that his initial relationship with the colonial governments in both Natal and the Cape were strained, would he have featured in a context where harsh colonial policies were enforced? His biographer and granddaughter, Margaret Rainier, often portrays him as sensitive to traditional issues and at loggerheads with the harsh colonial administration (Rainier 2002:104). While one probably needs to take for granted that, to be able to talk about agency, one has to assume that the agent had power, one may also consider the need for a conducive environment which assisted or made possible the exercise of that power. In this case, Madonella did acquire significant political, social, and even economic power, which one can assume to have assisted in the outcome of his efforts at linguistic mediation. There must have been other interpreters throughout the history of South Africa, but we have no record of them — or the records have not yet been found — because they may not have been as influential, i.e., powerful, as Madonella.

The relevance of Madonella's relationship with the Griqua can be illustrated by its relevance to current South African politics. Rainier quotes Dower who lamented the way in which the British Colonial government made "a huge mistake to trample on the feelings, the prejudices, and tender toes, of a whole people by the summary process adopted" (2002:68). She raises the matter of language and culture, arguing that a Dutch-speaking person like Madonella, who could communicate with the Griqua and who had spent more time with them than the British had, would perhaps have been better able to resolve problems between the Griqua and the British. She then refers to modern South African historians who lament the passing of the Griqua states as examples of societies which did not base themselves on color (Rainier 2002:68). To add to this picture, a modern academic, writing during the apartheid era, found it difficult to classify Madonella. He seems to have been too much of a hybrid, a border sample of humanity (Ross 1976:106):

> [Donald Strachan] more than anyone else, perhaps ... embodies the ambiguity
> of status which surrounds racial distinction in South Africa. Grandson [sic] of

> an immigrant from Scotland, he was genetically 'white' and was accepted as such
> … On the other hand … he became one of the most important figures in Griqua
> politics … To add to the difficulty of classifying him, he was a superb linguist,
> speaking all of the Bantu dialects of the area flawlessly, and was accepted as the
> leader of a 'regiment' of African tribesmen.

To my mind, Madonella's history should be studied in detail from the perspective
of encountering and representing the Other (Sturge 2007) with the aim of reflecting on current matters of border, hybridity, globalization, and, in South Africa,
nation building.

One can make a stronger case for his agency by looking at his views on matters
of race and culture. Rainier provides ample evidence of his "moderate" and even
sympathetic approach to indigenous people, a position which was not common
in South Africa in the mid-nineteenth century (Rainier 2002: 104, 106, 132–134).
I wish to underscore the complexity of the situation, however, by immediately
pointing out that Madonella later became a senator in the government of the Cape
Colony. Therefore, it would be impossible to call him an early post-colonialist.
Madonella himself was not oblivious to the border situation in which he lived.
In reports to the colonial government, he commented on the 'localization of the
law' (my term — KM) in depth (see Rainier 2002: 189–190). However, one cannot claim that he was assimilated or localized into traditional African societies
and their ways of living — there is too much proof of him remaining 'Western' at
heart. Nonetheless, his positions on acculturation and forcing Western values on
indigenous people were soft, for his time. I cannot part with the impression that
he acted from a generally sympathetic point of view because, once knowing the
language and custom of the Other, he could not think simply as an outsider/other.

Another question one has to ask is whether the loss of his roots played any
role in turning him into a figure that was able to cross borders? As a child, he lost
not only his parents but also his homeland. Did this lack of roots make it easier
for him to cross borders into other cultures? Madonella never commented on this
issue himself, and his biographer did not take it up. In a personal interview, I asked
this question to Snell, a teacher and historian in the Kokstad area. His response
(Snell 2010) was that it was possible but difficult to say definitively because there
is no evidence to it. Rainier also refers to Madonella's lack of reflection on his own
actions, typical of people acting to survive and not having the luxury of reflection.
Another perspective in this regard is quoted by Rainier (2002: 177–178). It is from
a correspondent writing in the Cape Argus on 22 February 1881:

> The whole body of natives in this part of the country, from the Umzimvubu to the
> Umzimkulu, are at his personal call, and without 'Madonella's' direction nothing
> effective will be done by them. He is a very chief, of themselves, yet vastly above

them all. He commands the respect of men of his own color just as much as he enjoys the confidence and esteem of the natives amongst whom his lot has been cast.

Apart from indicating his acceptance among various racial and cultural groups in a border situation, this quote hints at larger forces at work in his destiny by referring to his position as a lot that has been cast. His is indeed a complex case.

Was his language skill responsible for his insight into local peoples? In other words, can one generalize by saying that people knowing more than one language are usually more tolerant of other cultures, and thus more able to play mediating roles? Or was it perhaps his ability to work with people that led him to learning languages and their dialects? The question is in line with Gentzler's idea (2008: 183–187) of a psycho-social turn in Translation Studies. One could argue that it is the personality rather than the linguistic ability that was the driving factor (cause) behind someone like Madonella. Can one claim that it was his crossing of borders into the world of the locals, i.e., his empathy and understanding of the local, that made him view the harsh British colonial rule with suspicion? Or was it merely a pragmatic position for the sake of survival or financial gain? Perhaps pragmatism should be considered as a cause in the agency of translators. In another work by Snell (2000: 22–30), he notes that the farm on which Madonella's lived after 1874 was called Bizweni, which means "meeting place". This farm was used for meetings with various leaders from the area and testifies to Madonella's linguistic and political acumen. Playing devil's advocate, one could argue that a figure like Madonella could also have made use of interpreters, just as Adam Kok and the British colonial officials had done. Can one then conclusively prove that his linguistic skill made possible his influence and that he was an agent of social/cultural identity formation by means of his linguistic skill alone?

The following quote from his granddaughter's biography ascribes to Madonella a kind of agency that is similar to that described by most of the contributors to John Milton and Paul Bandia's (2009) volume on agency and translation.

> Umzimkulu lies on a multiple frontier. In the village and district extending along the south-western margin of the Great River from which they take their name, the currents of history swept together men and women differing widely in origin, language and culture, but fused towards the end of the nineteenth century into a cohesive and in many respects unique community. This was largely the result of the presence among them of Donald Strachan. (Rainier 2002: 1)

In terms of Sturge's (2007) theory, this representation is typical of the mono-voice anthropological writing, which she criticizes. Such writing contains a single voice, a single perspective, one story line — and inevitably, one conclusion. By representing Madonella from a number of perspectives, by posing a number of questions regarding the data we have available — always remembering that what we have is but a fraction of what happened, and already framed at that — I hope to illustrate the implications of Sturge's work for discussing agency in translation.

One needs to ask yet another question about agency: Can one ascribe unwitting agency to someone? All the examples in Milton and Bandia (2008) ascribe the agents as consciously, purposefully choosing a particular set of actions to achieve their goals. Can one say this of Madonella, or should one rather conclude that it is only in hindsight that one can call him an agent? Does that then render him not an agent? In the context in which he operated, survival could have been as important a motive for his actions as "agency." A letter from an associate, Harry Escombe, contains the following advice (Rainier 2002: 11):

> If you do business in Durban while I am away use my name with Muirhead and Co, Dickinson and Munro and the Standard Bank.

From this perspective, Madonella's motives for learning and using languages and dialects could have been quite selfish: the survival/advancement of his business initiatives. Snell (2005: 14–15) refers to this when reviewing complaints by fellow traders from that era, such as the following letter signed by G.P. Stafford, Darby and Tyrrel:

> We, the undersigned traders in Griqualand East would respectfully request to be placed upon an equal and as favorable footing as the firm of Messrs. Strachan and Co., which is not now the case in the present state of things.

When it comes to matters of agency, the perspective I wish to add is that determining agency is a complex matter. Milton and Bandia's collection of essays provides a number of case studies of people who were clearly agents of some kind of social project such as westernizing Japan, for which translation was an important tool. To me, the more difficult and thus more interesting cases are the people like Madonella, who used translation to achieve something, but the thing they achieved and their motives for it are much more difficult to pinpoint. As Jacobus Naudé's (2005) work on Bible translation shows, not all translators sit down to conceptualize a clear strategy for using translation to achieve a particular outcome, i.e. sometimes agency is an unintended consequence. Life is much too complex and messy to assume that everything that happens was planned. It seems to me that unintentional agency is part of translation action but that it is very difficult to prove a direct line of causality in such cases.

Lastly, one has to ask whether Madonella did indeed create a particular identity in the area. Translation Studies scholars such as Gentzler (2008) have argued that translators have the ability to create identity by the way in which they translate and by what they translate. What is at stake here is whether scholars are merely positing links between translators and identities, or whether they are able to prove those links. The debate on translation and identity could easily fall into a circular argument in which the conclusion is encapsulated in the assumption. How would one determine the link between translation action and identity in the case of Madonella, or in the case of any other translator for that matter? In my interview with Milner Snell, I asked him whether he would be able to point to the lasting effects of the influence of Madonella. He did not think it possible, although he was not sure (Snell 2010). Did Madonella's influence get lost in the mists of time? Was it only a very local influence tied to his personal history? Does one have to think about the creation of identity on a national scale only as was done by most articles in the work of Milton and Bandia (2008) and in the work of Gentzler, or could a number of localized identities add up to a national identity? In many contexts, it may not be feasible to indicate national or even regional identities as the result of translation. One may need to be happy with much more local findings. Furthermore, when it comes to intention, it becomes difficult to ascribe it to agents who were not intentional agents. Was it an ideal of a better world that drove Madonella or merely survival? That he played a significant role in his time and that his linguistic abilities contributed to him being able to cross borders in a way that even today catches the eye seems undeniable. But was it agency? And if so, what kind of agency? Gentzler and most other works on agency (Milton & Bandia 2008) and identity (Naudé 2005) study agency and identity at the level of literature or influential texts such as the Bible. Could the mere interpreting of a meeting be said to have the same influence?

Encountering Gentzler

Edwin Gentzler is a Translation Studies scholar working at the University of Massachusetts on the northern part of the East Coast of the USA. He has disseminated his work by means of journal articles, conference papers, and a number of books. In particular, this article provides a representation of his views on the "internationalization" of translation (Tymoczko 2008) and the agency role of translation as a force in the creation of identity as expressed in his latest book *Translation and identity in the Americas*. One may say that his effort to expand Translation Studies and to theorize the field using data from "other"[8] geopolitical areas is what makes him of interest to Africans like me. One may say that my interest in Gentzler is itself of a resistant nature: looking for theoretical constructs with which to resist dominant paradigms of thought in the field; or, put in a more positive light, looking for theoretical constructs by which to conceptualize the data

---

8. Used in the sense of Sturge (2007).

provided by the African context.[9] It is a matter of encounter, of being influenced while maintaining your identity, of reconsidering your identity while listening to the Other. It is a power struggle, involving assimilation and rejection.

As an African, I am interested in encountering Gentzler for a number of particular reasons. The following arguments from his book, I think, took root in my thoughts. The first is his argument that translation is not merely a mediator between existing cultures but an active force that creates culture. As he acknowledges, this is actually a refinement of the notion propagated by Susan Bassnett and Andre Lefevere (1995:5) nearly twenty years before him (also see Naudé 2005), that translation is a force which contributes to the formation of culture. Gentzler, however, focuses on the creation of identity. While translation is surely a formative force in the creation of identity, it is noticeable that Gentzler never defines identity. He posits the translational activity in the Americas as somehow creating an identity, mainly in opposition to European/colonial identities. One could venture as far as stating that Gentzler assumes that the effect of the type of translational action or inaction he describes creates identity without presenting a theory of how (cultural) identity is created. Bandia (2008) has made a similar point, namely, that the writing strategies of a number of African authors constitute, at least, resistance to colonialism or, at most, the creation of an African identity through resistance. Milton and Bandia (2009) take up the matter of agency but, once again, do not theorize agency in detail. These scholars present a largely historical description of agency roles played by particular people in particular contexts. While they focus on matters of patronage, power, habitus (Milton and Bandia 2009:2–10), planning (Even-Zohar 2008), and cultural agency (Tahir-Gürçağlar 2009), they fail to provide a clear causal connection (Chesterman 2000; 2008) between translational action and identity/culture. Or perhaps one should say, they view the connection at a sociological or planning level by looking at what Toury would call preliminary norms, choices concerning what to translate (Toury 1995). On the one hand, the connection between translation and identity has not been demonstrated to be strong, and on the other hand, culture and identity have been proven to be such elusive concepts that the arguments are not always convincing. To my mind, much more nuanced arguments are needed before translation scholars can claim agency in the construction of any kind of identity (see Naudé 2005 as an example).

---

9. The question here is whether what has been acknowledged as dominant paradigms of thought in Translation Studies — for which one may look at an introductory work such as that of Munday (2007) — are able to explain all the data from contexts in which these paradigms did not arise. In my interpretation, this is the main question asked by Tymoczko (2007) in her most recent work

A second point of interest in Gentzler's work is that he focuses exclusively on literary translation, as do most translation scholars working in the field of cultural translation and identity (see Bandia 2008; Milton and Bandia 2009). This raises the question as to whether the same would hold for the translation of pragmatic texts? It also raises the question of how representative that agency is. If one focuses on literary texts only, chances are that you will focus only on the creation of identity amongst the intellectuals in society. This is one reason why I have chosen for the first part of this case study not a literary figure but a political, economic, or social figure from the fringe of South African society and history. What Gentzler has awakened in me is the realization that Africa offers numerous cases of data other than those typical of high culture. The encounter with Gentzler has led me to the realization that his world is not my world. His book provided a mirror helping me to see my own world more clearly. Studying translational action in Africa cannot be restricted to literary translation or other features of the formal economy of the continent as is the current practice (see, for instance, the topics covered in the book of Judith Inggs and Libby Meintjes 2009).[10] In some of his earlier work, Gentzler (2001:x) stated that the rise of the developed world is a factor in the rise in translation activities because cultural, economic, social conditions determine the strategies for translation. The implication of this argument is that translation theorists in Africa need to refocus their interest urgently to include the developmental, informal, and communicative features of their context. Also, if one looks at how Michael Cronin (2008) connects translation to economic development, the next phase in Translation Studies needs to focus on the developmental context.

Third, Gentzler points to the growing realization that culture and identity are in themselves hybrid concepts. It may be that globalization has made us more aware of this point, but it has always been the case. Bandia (2008) has also written on hybridity, arguing that African literature is a hybrid between, at least, oral and written cultural ideas. Walter Ong (1995), basing his notions on the linguistic anthropology of Marcel Jousse[11] conceptualizes the hybridity of orality and literacy as secondary orality. Whichever way one looks at it, through numerous historical processes, of which colonization and globalization are perhaps the most obvious, African culture is of a hybrid nature. Alain Ricard and Flora Veit-Wild (2005) provide examples of not only hybridity in language but also in culture, themes of writing, and style of writing. Understanding hybridity, in particular, the hybridity

---

10. My criticism would here perhaps exclude Bandia's article, which seems to be looking widely at translation phenomena.

11. Much of Jousse's work has only recently been translated from the French, e.g., *The Anthropology of Geste and Rhythm* (Durban: Mantis Publishing, 2000), translated by Edgard Sienaert and Joan Conolly.

of developed and developing economies, formal and informal economies, is crucial for understanding and dealing with translation on the African continent.

Fourth, Gentzler points to the importance of the notion of border in current theorizing on translation.[12] Because translation happens at the point where cultures/languages meet, which is by definition some kind of border, and because globalization and colonization have changed the notion of borders, border is central to thought on translation in Africa. Africa has not only been subjected to the drawing of artificial borders, which has now opened up cross-border features in a number of fields, but South Africa is in itself a border. It has undergone a number of border wars and even has an area called "Border."[13] Its history is fraught with peoples/cultures encountering one another and having to deal with the Other and with difference. Apartheid was an ideology of borders ("good fences make good neighbors"). Migration is another response to this creation of borders, and it is a factor in translation that has not yet been studied in Africa. Furthermore, the Rainbow metaphor used by Archbishop Desmond Tutu still has a notion of borders, different colors, that seems to have been overcome in the one rainbow. However, the metaphor would not have been chosen if border was not a problem in South Africa. In this respect, I particularly wish to introduce Gentzler's theory to Madonella, someone living in a hybrid, border area in which at least five cultural/linguistic groups met. This could have been what Gentzler (2008:2), following Simon, calls a situation conducive to translation, i.e., the more borders, the more translation.

Fifth, Gentzler points out that one can, to some extent, read the formation of identity in parts of the Americas as a resistance to colonial identity. Except for the USA, which according to Gentzler has been shaped by non-translation, all other cultures in the Americas have been shaped by a resistant struggle against colonization. While Bandia (2008) has argued in favor of forms of resistance in translation/writing in Africa, as a South African, I am struck by translation into a language such as Afrikaans as an ambivalent form of resistance. On the one hand, Afrikaans, and its history and people, has built a name for itself as resisting English colonialism. Moreover, a substantial number of literary works have been translated into Afrikaans and other indigenous African languages, and the South African

---

12. Delabastita (2008:238) is critical of translation becoming a trope or metaphor for any experience of difference, change, unstable identities or secondariness. He calls for "strict rationality", indicating that the differences between Europe and America are becoming an epistemological breach. See also D'Hulst (2008). At this stage, I find myself on the side of America on this topic.

13. The area called "Border" roughly stretches from East London to Queenstown, a distance of about 200 km. It is situated in the current Eastern Cape Province and was the border between the white settlers and the Isixhosa.

Translator's Institute was founded in 1956 to promote the translation of pragmatic texts into Afrikaans.[14] Apart from Bible translation (Naudé 2005), however, very little evidence exists of resistant translation into Afrikaans or other African languages. As far as resistant translation in South Africa is concerned, I wish to posit a hypothesis, based on Gentzler's observations regarding South America, in order to stimulate similar studies in the African context. My hypothesis is that translations from European sources, rather than sources from other contexts, were preferred, and the translations were done in such a way that Europe was, in general, posited as the ideal society, not as a colonial power to be resisted. Very little literature from Africa has been translated into Afrikaans.[15] Because I view this article as exploring the implications that Gentzler may have for a research agenda for Translation Studies in Africa, I further posit the hypothesis, obviously to be tested against the data, that translation into Afrikaans served the purposes of recreating Europe in Africa. It seems that translation into Afrikaans only resisted the dominance of English over Afrikaans, which was part of the English policy of anglicization after the Anglo-Boer War. It did not resist colonization as such. It is thus a selective resistance, paradoxically resisting both English — by translation — and Africa — by non-translation. Resisting English was not resisting Europe. It was only resisting a particular, uncomfortable section of Europe.

A look at the web site of the currently popular Afro-French movement, in which the Department of Afrikaans, Dutch, French and German at the University of the Free State is involved, confirms this suspicion. Popular Afrikaans songs translated into French have recently sold 25 000 copies in a matter of months. The web site mentions the "nostalgia" of listening to well-known Afrikaans songs translated into French. To my mind, this is "resistant" translation — resisting the African context and continuing the colonial ideology fostered by white South Africans by feeding into an umbilical cord with Europe — and thus a continuation of the translation tradition of South Africa. At the same time, virtually nothing from the West of Africa, where French is the lingua franca, has been translated into Afrikaans. Gentzler (2008: 182–183) points out that gaps and silences are some of the major forces in shaping identity. He argues that the policy of non-translation in the USA has been instrumental in shaping the current identity of the USA. The lack of literary translations from African writers into Afrikaans and other African

---

14. See, for instance, De Kock's (2009) work on translations in South Africa.

15. In a current study by a master's student of mine, it took her four months of non-stop research to find Afrikaans translations of the Freedom Charter, on which the liberation struggle and the South African constitution were built. Those that she eventually found were in no way readily available. To my mind, this is another example of the historical metalepsis to which Gentzler (2008: 182–183) refers.

languages in South Africa is such a gap. To my mind, intra-continental translation in Africa is such a metalepsis.

Encountering the representation

Gentzler (2008: 180–187) closes his book by suggesting another turn in Translation Studies, a social-psychological one.[16] He argues that Translation Studies should focus on both the larger and the smaller picture (a similar suggestion has been made by his colleague, Maria Tymoczko (2002)). I have no qualms with this position as it seems to me to be a logical implication of developments in Translation Studies over the past decade, i.e., a simultaneous, seemingly contradictory, development toward both sociological, impersonal, macro-level factors and psychological, personal, micro-level factors.

After having juxtaposed the work of Madonella to that of Gentzler, I wish to suggest my own research program for Translation Studies in Africa — which may or may not have implications for Translation Studies outside of this context. For the sake of the coherence of my argument, I refer the reader back to my second footnote in which I set out my views on the notion of polemical writing. First, in following the example and suggestions made by the work of Gentzler and others, Translation Studies in (South) Africa needs to turn historical. By delving into its own history of translation, it will not only come of age as a discipline in its context, but it will also contribute to the global debate, finding its own voice rather than copying the voices of others. This is essentially a postcolonial, resistant position. It is also a postpositivist position, preferring some form of localized context, for the interim, ahead of a universal perspective or universal claims.

Second, Translation Studies in Africa needs to turn to technical or pragmatic texts. By this I mean that it has to turn its focus from studying the translation of literary texts exclusively to include the translation of technical or pragmatic texts.[17] As is the case in other continents, the bulk of translation work on the African continent lies on this level, and it has to be factored into studies on the creation of

---

16. I do not necessarily agree with yet another turn, as Translation Studies have seen numerous ones.

17. Defining non-literary texts is quite a problem. In her seminal work *Text Analysis in Translation*, Nord (2005: 21–22) uses the term non-literary. However, it has often been pointed out that defining something in terms of what it is not is not satisfactory. I thus use communicative or technical texts to indicate texts in which the main pragmatic function of the text is to communicate and literary texts to indicate texts in which the artistic creation is the main pragmatic function of the text.

identity and culture. The question that needs to be answered is whether the same claims that have been made for literary translation can also be made for pragmatic translation, involving the translation of economic, legal, and bureaucratic texts.

Third, Translation Studies in Africa needs to turn geographical. Gentzler's work actually makes a number of geographical or geopolitical assumptions. Translation Studies in Africa needs to consider matters such as aridity, rural locality, distance from centers of power, etc. which are usually factors of geography. For instance, what happens to interlingual communication in areas that are far from centers of power? Are there differences in interlingual communication practice between rural and urban areas, and if so, what is the nature of these differences?

Fourth, Translation Studies in Africa needs to turn informal. In South Africa, for example, it is estimated that between 15% and 30% of the economy is made up of the informal economy (UN Habitat 2006). Figures for the rest of Africa would be at least similar. By studying only the formal economy or formal features of the economy/society, Translation Studies is providing a skewed representation of the field or industry of Translation Studies. Up to this point in history, most studies on translation have focused on the formal economy. By turning the gaze of Translation Studies to informal economies, we can explore the extent to which the dominance of formal economies in the West has set a particular research agenda in Translation Studies.

Last, and most importantly, Translation Studies in Africa needs to turn developmental. I here refer both to development studies as a field of study and to development practice as a factor in constituting, among other things, the translation landscape in developing contexts. If what Gentzler, Tymoczko, and others have been advocating holds true, Translation Studies needs to turn its gaze to including the notion of development in its research agenda. Put differently, what would we find if we studied translation as a factor of development? What would we find if we studied development as a factor of translation? An example of this would be to study Madonella's views of and comments on legal localization as a case in translation (see Rainier 2002: 189). To my mind, the international turn in Translation Studies and the socio-psychological turn in Translation Studies argue for the fact that the differences between developed and developing contexts be factored into any notion of agency in Translation Studies. As a context, development cannot but be a factor in translation (Gentzler 2001: x). This interest has to become a focal point in Translation Studies in Africa — and may, I assume, become a focal point in studies of other developing contexts, as well.

Representing the encounter

I have represented my reading of Gentzler and my interpretation of the history of Madonella as an encounter of two Others. On purpose, I mixed my voice with theirs, making clear that they are a construct of my academic imagination, a narrative told to suit my purposes (Baker 2006). By mixing not only my voice with theirs, but also their voices with others who spoke about them, I hope to have represented an experiment in multiple voices in representing the encounter with the Other. The multiplicity or complexity of voices, however, goes further than the representation of my two guests. It goes to my writing this article in itself. I tried to represent the complexity of reading a Gentzler or a Madonella, subverting easy claims of causality between human agents and the effects, if any, that they have. I hope at least to have challenged some fixed notions of causality and to have suggested multiple causalities for the translation agency of Madonella, such as a particular context that may or may not have been conducive to translation, personal survival, economic survival, personality, linguistic ability, political acumen, and others. By juxtaposing these possible causes, I tried to subvert causality as the only principle in scientific discourse, allowing in theory, at least, the possibility of other, complex, unexplained relationships to be drawn between Madonella and aspects of his context. I tried to write a text that reflects on its reflection on reflection. I am asking whether it is at all possible for Madonella to be heard through all the representations. I tried to represent Gentzler in a coherent fashion, putting the more powerful Other in a theoretical box. I tried to represent Madonella as complex, trying to interpret him in a complex context. Or should it have been the other way round?

References

Afri-French. http://www.afrifrans.co.za. [Accessed on 28 May 2010].
Assman, Aleida. 1996. "The Curse and Blessing of Babel; or, Looking Back at Universalisms." In *The Translatability of Cultures: Figurations of the Space Between*, edited by Sanford Budick and Wolfgang Iser, 85–100. Stanford: Stanford University Press.
Baker, Mona. 2006. *Translation and Conflict. A Narrative Account.* New York: Routledge.
Bandia, Paul. 2009. "Translation Matters: Linguistic and Cultural Representation." In *Translation Studies in Africa*, edited by Judith Inggs and Libby Meintjes, 1–20. London: Continuum.
Balson, Scott. 2007. *Children of the mist: The lost tribe of South Africa.* Queensland: Interactive Presentations.
Bassnett, Susan and Lefevere, André (eds). 1995. *Constructing Cultures: Essays on Literary Translation.* Clevedon: Multilingual Matters.

Chesterman, Andrew. 2000. "A Causal Model for Translation Studies." In *Intercultural Faultlines. Research Models in Translation Studies I: Textual and Cognitive Aspects*, edited by Maeve Olohan, 15–28. Manchester: St Jerome.

Chesterman, Andrew. 2008. "The Status of Interpretive Hypotheses." In *Efforts and Models in Interpreting and Translation Research*, edited by Gyde Hansen, Andrew Chesterman, and Heidrun Gerzymisch-Arbogast, 49–62. Amsterdam: Benjamins.

Cronin, Michael. 2008. "Downsizing the World. Translation and the Politics of Proximity." In *Beyond Descriptive Translation Studies. Investigations in Homage to Gideon Toury*, edited by Anthony Pym, Miriam Shlesinger and Daniel Simeoni, 265–276. Amsterdam: Benjamins.

De Kock, Leon. 2009. "Cracking the Code: Translation as Transgression in Triomf." In *Translation Studies in Africa*, edited by Judith Inggs and Libby Meintjes, 21–43. London: Continuum.

Delabastita, Dirk. 2008. "Status, Origin, Features. Translation and Beyond." In *Beyond Descriptive Translation Studies. Investigations in Homage to Gideon Toury*, edited by Anthony Pym, Miriam Shlesinger and Daniel Simeoni, 233–246. Amsterdam: Benjamins.

D'Hulst, Lieven. 2008. "Cultural Translation: A Problematic Concept?" In *Beyond Descriptive Translation Studies. Investigations in Homage to Gideon Toury*, edited by Anthony Pym, Miriam Shlesinger and Daniel Simeoni, 221–232. Amsterdam: Benjamins.

Even-Zohar, Itamar. 2008. "Culture Planning, Cohesion and the Making and Maintenance of Entities." In *Beyond Descriptive Translation Studies. Investigations in Homage to Gideon Toury*, edited by Anthony Pym, Miriam Shlesinger and Daniel Simeoni, 277–292. Amsterdam: Benjamins.

Gentzler, Edwin. 2001. *Contemporary Translation Theories*. Revised 2nd edition. Clevedon: Multilingual Matters Ltd.

Gentzler, Edwin. 2008. *Translation and Identity in the Americas. New Directions in Translation Theory*. London: Routledge.

Hermans, Theo. 2007. *The Conference of the Tongues*. Manchester: St Jerome.

Houtondji, Paul. 1996. *African Philosophy. Myth and Reality*. 2nd edition. Bloomington: Indiana University Press.

Inggs, Judith and Meintjes, Libby. 2009 . Introduction. In *Translation Studies in Africa,* edited by Judith Inggs and Libby Meintjes, xii–xviii. London: Continuum.

Jousse, Marcel. 2000. *The Anthropology of Geste and Rhythm*. Translated by Edgard Siennaert and Joan Connoly. Durban: Mantis Publishing.

Milton, John and Bandia, Paul. 2009. *Agents of Translation*. Amsterdam: Benjamins.

Munday, Jeremy. 2007. *Introducing Translation Studies: Theories and Applications*. London: Routledge.

Naudé, Jacobus. 2005. "The Afrikaans Bible Translations and the Formation of Cultural, Political and Religious Identities in South Africa." In *Translation and the Construction of Identity*, edited by Juliane House, Rosario Martín Ruano, and N. Baumgarten, 167–179. IATIS Yearbook.

Nord, Christiane. 2005. *Text Analysis in Translation: Theory, Methodology, and Didactic Application of a Model for Translation-Oriented Text Analysis*. 2nd edition. Translated by C. Nord and P. Sparrow. Amsterdam: Rodopi.

Ong, Walter. 1995. *Orality and Literacy. The Technologizing of the Word*. Routledge: New York.

Pym, Anthony. 1998. *Method in Translation History*. Manchester: St Jerome.

Rainier, Margaret. 2002. *Madonella. Donald Strachan — Autocrat of Umzimkulu*. North End: CADAR.

Ricard, Alain & Veit-Wild, Flora (eds). 2005. *Interfaces between the Oral and the Written/ Interfaces entre l'écrit et l'oral. Versions and Subversions in African Literatures* 2. Amsterdam: Rodopi.

Ross, Robert. 1976. *Adam Kok's Griquas.* Cambridge: Cambridge University Press.

Snell, Milner. 2000. *Early Settler Families at Umzimkulu: 1854–1884.* Kokstad.

Snell, Milner. 2005. *Strachan & Co. (Pty) Limited.* Kokstad.

Snell, Milner. 2010. "Personal Interview Conducted at Kokstad on 14 May 2010."

Sturge, Kate. 2007. *Representing Others: Translation, Ethnography and the Museum.* Manchester: St Jerome.

Tahir-Gürçağlar, Şehnaz. 2009. "A cultural agent against the forces of culture: Hasan-Âli Yücel". In: Agents of translation, edited by John Milton and Paul Bandia. Amsterdam: Benjamins.

Tymoczko, Maria. 2002. "Connecting the Two Infinite Orders: Research Methods in Translation Studies." In *Crosscultural Transgressions. Research Models in Translation Studies II: Historical and Ideological Issues,* edited by Theo Hermans, 9–25. Manchester: St Jerome.

Tymoczko, Maria. 2007. *Enlarging Translation, Empowering Translators.* Manchester: St Jerome.

UN-HABITAT. 2006. *Innovative Policies for the Urban Informal Economy.* UNHSP. Nairobi: UN-HABITAT.

On fictional turns, fictionalizing twists and the invention of the Americas

Roberto A. Valdeón

In his 2008 book, *Translation and Identity in the Americas*, Edwin Gentzler proposed a "fictional turn" to refer to translation in connection with the construction of identity in the Americas, a highly positive view of the role played by this activity since the arrival of the Europeans. This paper proposes a "fictionalizing twist," that is, a complementary approach that would attest to the less positive use of translation in the relation between Europe and the Americas on the one hand, and among European nations on the other. Thus, I examine how translation and Translation Studies have contributed to creating certain negative images of translators and nations, a tendency that can still be traced nowadays. First, I discuss the views on the indigenous interpreter Malinche and her part in the conquest of Mexico. Then I move on to examine the ideological manipulation of texts used to promote antagonistic national identities within the European context at the time. Finally, it is argued that both the fictional turn and the fictionalizing twist need to be considered as an integral part of the identity-construction process in the Americas and in Europe.

Introduction

In 2008 Edwin Gentzler called for a "fictional turn" with regards to translation and the formation of identity in Latin America. He claimed that "Translation in South America is much more than a linguistic operation; rather, it has become one of the means by which an entire continent has come to define itself" (2008: 108). Contentious as the claim might be in a discipline that has been exposed to continuous "turns" (Snell-Hornby 2006), Gentzler's suggestion remains powerful in a continent whose identity has been shaped via translation, and not merely via the translation of fiction. Translation as a topic in fiction, the translation of European thinkers, and translation in the historical construction/destruction of empires have also made an impact upon the continent.

Gentzler's discussion of the "fictional turn" draws on both the representation of translation in Latin American literature and on the assumptions that readers can make with regards to translation as reflected by fiction writers. His discussion involves Borges (2008: 110–119), García Márquez (119–123) and Vargas Llosa (124–130) as well as Derrida and Benjamin (130–136), and highlights the power of translation in a continent that attempts to define itself in terms of its European origins but also of its native roots. Translation is not so much about rendering an existing text into a different language, but about opening and, to some extent, creating new worlds for new audiences. Thus, translators contribute to shaping identity in the Americas by "drawing upon the local in the target culture" (2008: 114), by emphasizing that "translation is as creative as original writing" (2008: 115), by adapting rather than adopting (2008: 134). Gentzler adds that American identity "is caught upon images of exploration, development, expansion, and renewal" (2008: 133). Translation can have a liberating force capable of undermining the power of colonial Europe upon the hemisphere. That is to say, the "fictional turn" might contribute to dismantling Eurocentrism in the Americas.

In this paper I would like to expand on the role of translation in the relationship between Europe and the Americas, drawing upon this controversial "turn" by taking it further, and, thus, examining the backflow of translation upon the formation of identities in the Americas as well as in Europe. The first point that deserves attention at the outset is the concept of Eurocentrism itself, which, in the Humanities and the Social Sciences, has been challenged as theoretically unclear: "[It] does not suggest a particular methodological approach to modernity, it is best seen in the context of a reflexive discourse of anti-Eurocentrism entailing to varying degrees a critique of the West and in particular a critique of ideologies that distort the relation of the West to the rest of the world" (Delanty 2006). As a working definition, I might well use Rabasa's approach to the concept. In his view it is not "simply a tradition that places Europe as a universal cultural ideal embodied in what is called the West, but rather a pervasive condition of thought" (1993: 18).

Domingues relates it to the controversy concerning whether Latin American nations can be considered part of the West, and even if they should aim at that. He quotes Sarmiento, one of the founding fathers of Argentina, as saying that Argentineans had to choose between "barbarism" and "civilization", but waged several wars against Europeans (including Iberian heritage) (2006: 379). Some years later Uruguay's Rodó regarded European immigrants as representatives of Shakespeare's Caliban and aligned himself with the more intellectual Prospero. However, during the Cuban revolution, Caliban symbolized the people oppressed by European colonialism and the struggle for liberation. The contradiction remains very much unsolved (Domingues 2006: 379).

Domingues believes that what is at stake here is the issue of identity, which has been linked to the modernization (or Westernization) of the American nations. Nowadays, he argues, modernization is very much a North American construct, which, despite its "totally discredited intellectual bias, still dominates much of 'Latin American' studies" (2006: 385). He claims that, to some extent, modernity has brought about an illusion of the dispersion of Eurocentric power. It is true that the 19th and 20th centuries meant a shift from the core (as represented by Europe) to other areas, to the periphery. But while some are clearly not Western (but have succumbed to Western influence), Latin America is within a Eurocentric sphere, now represented by North America (Domingues 2008: ix). Thus, there is no clear dilution of the concepts of core and periphery with regards to Eurocentrism (Domingues 2006: 389).

Harris mentions that Eurocentrism is vital to understanding the nationalist movements that would give rise to the emergence of the Colombian or Mexican nations (2006: 45), while Moreiras (1999) underscores that the concept serves the purpose of creating an alternative approach to literature, not so much derived from the European traditions as from American experience. Latin American literature cannot escape its obvious European cultural roots or "obvia matriz cultural eurocéntrica" (1999: 55 & 70), but by rejecting it, writers manage to create their own sense of identity. Thus anti-Eurocentrism is a convenient concept to promote a certain sense of unity, of uniformity. Both Eurocentrism and anti-Eurocentrism can be regarded as narratives created, that is invented, to sustain another narrative, that of an American identity. Academics in the Americas also recognize the influence of European thinkers and scholars upon Latin America and the construction if its identity. Szurmuk & McKee, for instance, stress that "translation contributed to the appropriation of European thinkers even before they made an impact on their northern neighbours" (2009: 14). In their view translation has played an ambivalent role in the Americas, since it often reflected European paradigms and imposed the European literary canon upon the new readership. However, they also stress that Latin American writers turned the illusion into authenticity by pretending that translation played a role in recovering old Latin American traditions. Translation of the oral literary traditions contributed to a new narrative with deep roots in the continent: "Se recuperaba, vía la oralidad, esa parte de la identidad latinoamericana que el canon literario había excluído" (2009: 201), that is, it helped recover the oral traditions of Latin America often excluded by the literary canon.

This symbiosis between the European and the native has been discussed by Brazilian translation scholars (and others) within the so-called cannibalist approach. The origins of the term "Cannibalism" are unclear, as Milton and Bandia point out (2009: 12). Although the concept originated in the 1920s

(Munday 2001:36; Milton & Bandia 2010:12) in Oswald de Andrade's *Manifesto Antropófago*, it was not until the 1990s that it began to be widely used in Translation Studies, first by Else Vieira, then by Susan Bassnett and Edwin Gentzler (Milton & Bandia 2010:12). Bassnett argues that "the horror aroused by cannibalism in the European imagination has been a recurring motif in the work of many writers from the sixteenth century onwards" (2010:85), but cannibalistic translators, like cannibalistic writers, seek "to reclaim a language that has been imposed upon their culture" (2010:84). In this sense, and unlike the European tradition, cannibalism has a positive component that combines "aspects of European presence without forgetting native traditions, forms, and meanings" (Gentzler 2008:79). Gentzler, who has written extensively on the issue (2008:77–107), puts emphasis on the cannibalistic approach as reelaboration (2008:78), rewriting and reinterpreting (2008:79), positive as a whole, but also acknowledges the ambivalence of the term vis-à-vis the European views on cannibalism (2008:78).

From a fictional turn to the fictionalizing twist

The ambivalent role of translation is of particular interest not only in the construction of identity in the Americas, but also in Europe. It is a role that transcends the fictional turn as proposed by Gentzler, and before him by Vieira (quoted by Gentzler 2008:132–133) and Larkosh (2004:33), because it does not merely connect translation to the literary traditions of Europe and the oral traditions of the Americas. It does not rely solely on the representations of reality in fiction or the narration of experience (Gentzler 2008:137). And it is not only about the "way representations of translators and interpreters in literature and both intellectual and popular culture has had an enormous power to shape public perceptions or misconceptions regarding the necessity and value of work in translation and interpretation" (Larkosh 2004:33), but also about the conceptual representations of interpreters and translators by academia. This role has been fictionalized to fit in with preconceived epistemological approaches and has made an impact upon the perception of the role of translators in the shaping of identity in the Americas.

Thus, the fictional turn has a fictionalizing twist, whereby fiction and translation meet in images of expansion, exploration and development (Gentzler 2008:133). This twist is not unknown in the stories that tell us the history of the continent. Some historians have used the phrase the "invention of America" to refer to the formation of an American identity (O'Gorman 1958, Rabasa 1993; Restall 2003:102). This is a concept that is related to what we can also call the American paradox, a continent at the crossroads between cultures and languages, striving to create an identity that is partly its own, partly inherited from the

European nations that settled down from the 16th century onwards. This paradox, which has been noted by critics, social scientists, and historians, is sustained by the perception of Europe as a cohesive geopolitical power capable of organizing itself to invent this New World. The notion of invention, as used by Rabasa in his study on the relationship between the Americas and Europe "first appeared in the title of a book by Hernández Pérez de Oliva, *Historia de la invención de las Yndias* (c. 1528), where the term *invención* reflects the Latin inuenire, to discover" (Rabasa 2002:3). The term was later used by Mexican historian Edmundo O'Gorman, author of *La invención de América*, who argued that America was not discovered but invented. He rejected the idea used by previous historians that America was a mistake, and claimed that the Europeans needed to interpret a reality they were unable to comprehend. O'Gorman mentions that the Vatican issued a decree granting the Spanish crown the rights over the lands defined as the Western part of the ocean towards the Indies. The *Inter Caetera* decree, as it was known, was passed in 1493 (O'Gorman 2003:89). O'Gorman questions the notion of discovery on a philosophical basis, but he underlines that the *idea* of the discovery might have been favoured from as early as 1494.

Rabasa retains the concept of *invention* and relates it to translation as an example of the asymmetric relationship between the Europeans and Amerindians. "There is only dialogue among the same, and indeed, it is power-ridden. Since going native forecloses the possibility of representing the other, control by means of translation seems to be the other alternative. Logical as well as rhetorical constructs, however, thwart the project of translation" (Rabasa 1993:92). This seems to imply that Europeans were better informed than Native Americans and, therefore, could use that extra knowledge for their own benefit. Restall underlines that there is no evidence that this was the case (2003:91). Translation, thus, becomes part of the paradox that characterizes the New World where historic figures and facts have been fictionalised and have contributed to the invention of both the Americas and Europe. In the next section I will examine how a historical figure has played a major role in the invention of a narrative, albeit a conceptual one, that has contributed to the shaping of identity in the Americas: the translator as a traitor.

Fictionalizing the interpreter

Translation has contributed to the emergence of invented narratives about the Other: the Europeans about the Amerindians but also the other way around. For instance, anthropologist Olivia Harris believes that, initially, Amerindians might have paid little attention to the arrival of Europeans: for instance the Mexican Selden Codex of Mixteca, which covers the years of the Spanish arrival, makes no mention of the strangers (Harris 2006: 42). Harris makes the case that translation may have been instrumental in the invention of the Europeans as gods or semi-gods. Like Rabasa (1993: 110–112), she argues that it is unclear whether the indigenous populations of the Americas believed the Spaniards to be gods. In the case of the Aztecs, the interpreter used by the Spaniards might have been partly responsible for this. Felipillo, as he was known, must have had difficulties to presenting the Spanish to the natives and may have attempted to describe them as Christians, that is, the "sons of God". If the phrase was rendered as "the sons of Viracocha", this could explain the identification between the Europeans and gods, that is, in terms of ambiguous linguistic transfer rather than in terms of the ignorance of the natives (Harris 2006: 39–40). But Harris casts doubts over whether the native elites would have taken the Spaniards for gods, and emphasizes that it was the local power struggles that probably played a significant role in the success of the conquerors (Harris 2006: 42).

The conquest (with the destruction that this entails) and the invention of America are contentious issues that have bewildered and antagonized historians. Contemporary studies on the arrival of the Europeans attempt to accommodate facts and figures that, as a result of the carefully constructed national narratives of the 17th and 18th centuries, were often unaccounted for. Acknowledging the destruction brought about by the arrival of the Europeans, Kamen states that probably "the element of conquest in the empire was small (...) Their feats have often been mythified as a victory of few over many, of European arms and expertise over primitive cultures. The success of the conquistadors was in reality no mystery. Both Pizarro and Cortés were fortunate in being able to exploit the state of civil dissention in the American empires" (2001: 153). Damrosh reminds us that, prior to the conquest, the common people of Mesoamerica had never participated in the wealth and power enjoyed by the nobility: "This is not to say that the entire population didn't suffer severely, particularly as disease and mistreatment led to a shocking loss of life" (Damrosh 2003: 99), but the already-existing oppression persuaded many native groups to cooperate with the Spaniards. More recently a number of historians have attempted to provide a more comprehensive view of the invasion/invention of America (Powell 1971;[1] Kagan 2002; Restall 2003). In fact,

---

1. Powell was among the first Anglophone historians to suggest the need for a new approach to Spain and Hispanic countries, particularly within the US. Although his book was controversial at the time and has remained so (it has recently been recommended by some ultraconservative media in Spain), Powell is a respected figure at the University of California, where he founded one of the first majors in Hispanic Civilization in the nation. His book is still recommended reading by the Organization of American Historians. Powell attempted to pull down the prejudice barriers held in his country against Spain and Latin America. Even if some of the arguments he used in his book are controversial, recent events in the US, such as the attitude towards the

even militant historians like Zinn have acknowledged that human loss and destruction were not unknown in the Americas before the arrival of the Europeans
(Zinn 2003:11), even if it was somehow "innocent".

The invention of the continent can be traced in the portrayal of one of the
translators of the period, Doña Marina, Hernán Cortés's interpreter. Doña Marina,
or La Malinche as she is also known, epitomizes the fictionalization of the translator in order to support specific (and often antagonistic) conceptual narratives.
And yet, as has been noted (Restall 2003:88), this is quite surprising for someone
who died very young. Doña Marina has been regarded as much a traitor as a translator (Todorov 1999:100; González 2002; Sten 2003:135–136; Núñez 2006:154).
Tzvetan Todorov believes that Doña Marina not only translated, but also adopted
all the Spanish ways (1999:101) as reflected by the fact that Cortés himself held
her in such esteem that he turned her into his lover. However, in his accounts of
the conquest, the Spaniard made only two occasional references to her (Restall
2003:87). So why did La Malinche become such an icon, unlike other interpreters
who served for much longer periods and, no doubt, had a greater command of the
language? Probably, as Restall points out, because she symbolizes many things at
once: betrayer, a sexual siren, a feminist symbol, the mother of the nation, and the
ultimate victim of rape (Restall 2003:86).

In fact, this multiplicity has been the base for the construction/invention of
her identity within translation studies. She has inspired extremely negative interpretations of her role as an intercultural communicator. Lefevere (1995:148),
Bassnett & Trivedi (1999:4), Arrojo (1999) and Baker (2009) have been particularly critical of her figure. As recently as in 2009, Baker stressed the role of La
Malinche as a traitor to her own people, "because Malinche (Doña Marina), who
interpreted for Hernán Cortés in the early sixteeth century, was heavily implicated
in his colonial schemes, acting as an informant and warning him of ambushes by
her people" (2009:xvi).

Arrojo argues that "to this day, her name is a sad reminder of the Spaniards'
brutal violation of the land and of the women of Mexico, 'passively open' to the
invader's power and cruelly abandoned to their faith after being used and exploited" (1999:142). Arrojo quotes Octavio Paz to establish that the Mexican identity
is based on the binary opposition "the vulnerable" versus "the invulnerable". The
former are "associated with the feminine, the open, the weak, the violated, the
exploited, the passive, the insulted" and the latter "associated, of course, with the
masculine, the closed, the aggressive, the powerful, capable of hurting and humili-
ating" (Arrojo 1999:142). But, even if in *El laberinto de la soledad* (*The Labyrinth of*

---

massive influx of immigrants from South of the border and the "threat" of Spanish as the second
language, among many other issues, show that much needs to be done.

Solitude) Octavio Paz referred to the paradox of La Malinche as being at the root of the Mexican identity vis-à-vis the European conqueror, he also concluded that the Mexican people were unable to come to terms with their own mixed identity because of their inability to accept their own historical predicament (1997: 110–112), much more a result of the mixture of cultures than in the case of North America, where the indigenous component has been practically wiped out.

Other writers have attempted to either understand her predicament as a woman and a cultural mediator, or have openly exposed the "invention" of the character that might well fit into a certain narrative, but does not necessarily correspond to a historical account of her figure and her role in the conquest. Simon underlines that, despite the negative associations of the character, she has the "honor of being one of the few women who is remembered for her work as a cultural intermediary" (1996: 40). The contradiction surrounding this character is demonstrated in Baker's collected volume (2009), where one of the contributors provides a different approach to her figure. Delabastita uses Doña Marina as an example of "the problems of interlinguistic and intercultural mediation in colonial settings" (2009: 111). In his view, the fictionalization of the interpreters has created a number of competing narratives "some of which have gone on to lead a life of their own as powerful myths in the grey zone between fact and fiction" (2009: 111) and, in fact, many voices reclaim her "as a national figure, worthy of respect because of her linguistic abilities and intelligence" (Aranda 2007: 29).

Zuñiga stresses the ability of La Malinche to translate between cultures (2003: 64) whereas González, for instance, provides us with information about the procedures La Malinche is likely to have used when interpreting between the Amerindians and the Europeans, and underlines her ability to adapt the words of Cortés to the native polysystem, as we might call it today (2002: 144ff). Sten has suggested that La Malinche might have been in command of the situation (Sten 2003: 137–139). After all she was fluent in two Amerindian languages and Spanish. She probably had to make a great effort to culturally substitute concepts that must have been very difficult to render: Spanish was more direct whereas the other two languages were far more ritual.

In any case, what is more interesting is the transformation of the historical figure into a fictional character that has given rise to many contradictory interpretations. La Malinche has been a traitor, a slave, a concubine, but also a fighter, an intermediary, an invention. The paradox reappears as the connecting thread between fiction and reality, the Europeans and the indigenous, the invisibility and the struggle for an identity. As Núñez has underlined, La Malinche is a product of the invasion (2006: 154), and as such she promoted the invention of America for the Europeans who saw through her eyes and mouth. Bernal Díaz del Castillo described her as the tongue of the conquest (1963: 86–87), an invisible counsellor that vanished as soon as, back in Spain, Cortés married into the aristocracy.

Todorov, however, prefers to regard her as an intermediary, as the result of a symbol of "the cross-breeding of cultures" (1999: 101). But we can go beyond the limitations of La Malinche the interpreter, and realize that, as a human being who was sold by her own people (Socolow 2000: 34–35), and as (most likely) an intelligent woman that did not fit into contemporary conceptions of national, social or even gender identity, she had to survive in rather harsh circumstances in both pre and post-Columbian America. In this respect it comes as no surprise to see that La Malinche has been appropriated and reinterpreted by many Chicano feminist writers who regard her as a painful example of their own predicament, torn between worlds: the indigenous and the European, but also between their countries of origin and their Anglophone adopted land (Alarcón 2006: 147–148). For example, in her book *Palabras de mediodía*, Lucha Corpi is inspired by the traditional imaginary of Doña Marina in a series of poems that also cast her in a new light. She is presented as a woman that anticipates a transformation born out of her own historical, social and economic predicament:

> Ella (Marina ausente)
> Ella. Una flor quizá, un remanso fresco…
> una noche tibia, tropical,
> o una criatura triste, en un una prisión
> encerrada: de barro húmedo y suave:
> es la sombra enlutada de un recuerdo
> ancestral que vendrá por la mañana
> cruzando el puente con manos llenas –
> llenas de sol y tierra.[2] (Corpi 2001: 124)

Telling it how it was?: Translation, history and the invention of the Americas / Europe

One of the reasons why Doña Marina has been fictionalized to such an extent is, no doubt, that there are no traces of her words, but rather recollections by third parties who had an interest in presenting her in a given light. Restall has rightly talked about the lost words of La Malinche (2003: 77–99). This section examines

---

2. The English version runs along these lines: She (Marina Distant) / She. A flower, a pool of fresh water… / a tropical night, / or a sorrowful child, enclosed / in a prison of the softest clay: / mourning shadow of an ancestral memory, crossing the bridge at daybreak, her hands full of earth and sun." (2001: 125).

the *not lost* words of the witnesses of the conquest, and more precisely those of Fray Bartolomé de las Casas, the Dominican friar who became an impassioned defender of Indian rights through the monumental *Historia de las Indias* and, above all, *Brevíssima relación de la destruyción de las Indias*, the tract that he wrote to advise crown prince Phillip of Spain on how to administer the colonies and put an end to the destruction of the lands. The text epitomized the confrontation between Europe and the Americas and, ultimately, shaped national identities in Europe. The effects of the text and its translations can be traced in the emergence of the Black Legend that characterized Spain as an evil nation, responsible for the destruction in the Americas and the political unrest in Europe at the time.

In the 16th and 17th centuries the promotion of narratives based on the fierce destruction of the Other used the Americas as a cornerstone, often via translation or adaptation, and the tradition lived on for many centuries to come. The Anglo-Spanish rivalry is a case in point. At the turn of the 20th century, English historian John Green reminded us of its survival as he defended England's anti-Spanish feelings. In his *Short History of the English People* Green justified "the old English hatred of Spain" (Green 1895:592). The British historian defined the Southern rival in the following terms: "Spain was at this moment the mightiest of European powers (...) the Spanish generals stood without rivals in their ruthless cruelty" (1895:411). "The shadow of this gigantic power", he continued, " felt like a deadly blight over Europe" (1895:411), reminiscent of the Black Legend that had swept across Europe, notably the Low Countries and England, in the 16th and 17th centuries, proving that it remained very much in the imaginary of the English. In fact, it was very much at the root of the emergence of an English identity within the European context.

Much of the information upon which historians like Green based their accounts had originated in the Low Countries, and had been translated into English to create the anti-Spanish sentiment necessary for the justification of British imperialism. Brinton mentions the case of Chilmead's translated versions of Thomas Campanella's *Spanish Monarchy*, a series of pamphlets that attempted to spread "sensationalized instances of Spanish cruelty" (Brinton 2009:81). Pincus adds that the translations of Campanella's work, which was a "treatise as a form of advice from afar to Philip III" in order to promote a universal monarchy (1996:185), were often expurgated versions aiming to emphasise the evil of Spain.

However, the most interesting example of translated propaganda in the period can be found in the various English versions of the tract by the Dominican friar Bartolomé de las Casas. Las Casas had been working in the Americas for many years and witnessed the good and, more often, the evil of the arrival of Europeans. Critical of so much destruction, "he became the early modern era's most articulate defender of the Indian rights" (Donovan 1992:2), and wrote a tract to advise the crown prince on how to deal with the situation in the Americas after his accession to the throne. Although Las Casas was the source of inspiration of a more romanticized approach to the Hispanic World, i. e. that of Washington Irving's *A History of the Life and Voyages of Christopher Columbus* (Adorno 2002: 60–61), he contributed to the construction of the Black Legend through the adaptations of his *Brevísima relación de la destrucción de las Indias*. The tract was published in Spain, and rapidly rendered into the major European languages of the time, Flemish, French, German and Latin and, in 1583, into English from a previous French version. *The Spanish Colonie*, was printed in London for William Brome. Consequently, the English exploited the concept of the Spanish "Black Legend" as constitutive of the Spanish identity (Donovan 1992: 9; Thomas 1993: 69; Brinton 2009: 51) as opposed to the good-heartedness and honesty of the English.

The text gave way to two more versions (Brinton 2009: 81) under very different titles, the most notable of which was *Tears of the Indians, being a historical Account of the Cruel Massacres and Slaughters of Above Twenty Millions of Innocent People, Committed by the Spaniards in the Islands of Hispaniola, Cuba, Jamaica & c. as also, in the Continent of Mexico, Peru, & other Palces of the West-Indies, to the total destruction of those Countries* (1656), indicative of the narrative that the translator attempted to construe. Particularly noticeable is the evaluative tone of the adjectives and the precise reference to numbers in the title. Thus, the translations of Las Casas's work served as one basis for the "so-called Black Legend, which sought to discredit Spain's American involvement by painting all Spanish activities and the Spanish national character in the most cruel and negative light" (Donovan 1992: 2). Frohock believes that this translation or adaptation results in the "British demonization of the Spanish" (2004: 30) in order to promote the colonial discourse of the English, who would act "through the goodness and providence of God" to avenge the Indians "so barbarously butchered by the Spaniards" (Cromwell's Declaration, quoted by Frohock 2004: 32) .

Written by John Phillips, a nephew of John Milton, this work had a long-lasting influence on the invention of Spain as intrinsically evil and on the formation of national identities in Europe. Phillips's version of the *Brevísima* (literally "extremely short [account]") contributed to fictionalizing an account that had been fictionalized from its inception. I am not referring to the facts and figures of the book. These have been the object of much controversy up to the present. In fact, whereas some scholars take the words of the friar literally (Stannard 1992; Zinn 2003) or defined them as "remarkably accurate (and often, in quantitative terms, even underestimates)" (Stannard 1992: 98), other writers equally critical of the conquest believe Las Casas was no historian and, as such, was not interested in providing accurate figures (Rabasa 1993; Restall 2003). He probably aimed to denounce "the dimensions of the destruction" rather than provide an "accurate census" (Rabasa 1993: 197), which, in any case, he would have been unable to do. In fact, Rabasa stresses the role of Bartolomé de las Casas, and also of other participants in the conquest, in the invention of America for the Europeans. Las Casas produced a narrative that needed to fit into preconceived images of the world, not merely geographical, but also social, religious, economic and cultural. It did not matter that Las Casas might have exaggerated many events and simply omitted others (no mention is made, for instance, to the diseases taken by the Europeans, which decimated the population). But even if we leave aside the controversial figures, his descriptions of the Caribbean islands clearly idealized the reality he had encountered. The following passage is indicative of the imaginary he created for his intended reader, as indicated, crown prince Phillip of Spain:

> Había en esta isla Española cinco reinos muy grandes principales y cinco reyes muy poderosos (…) entran en ella sobre treinta mil ríos y arroyos, entre los cuales son los doce tan grandes como Ebro y Duero y Guadalquivir; y todos los ríos que vienen de la una sierra que está al Poniente, que son los veinte y veinticinco mil, son riquísimos de oro… (Las Casas 2009: 20)

These images must have made an impact on the political élite and influenced the political decisions of other European powers. In these cases, Phillips's version remains close to the original:

> *The island of Hispaniola had in it five very great Kingdomes, and five very potent Kings (…) it is watered by thirty thousands Rivers and Rivolets, whereof twelve are not lesse than either Duerus, Ebrus, or Gualgevir; and all the Rivers which run from the mountains on the West side, whose number is twenty thousand, do all of them abound with gold.* (Phillips 1656: 11)

These representations were, no doubt, instrumental in the promotion of Eurocentric perceptions of the world, but also contributed to the construction of the antagonistic national identities in Europe, as can be traced in the preface, where Phillips portrays the Spanish by resorting to words like "satanical", "cruelties" and "barbarous", whereas "honour" and "purity" were attached to the people of his native England. When Phillips eventually starts his translation, he makes sure that the scope and strength of the account is not only maintained but clearly intensified. Most passages are modified to construe the narrative of the evil Other and justify English intervention in the Americas. Whereas Las Casas is critical of the unchristian ways of the Spaniards, Phillips tends to avoid the reference to Christianity and chooses nouns or adjectives denoting nationality (Spanish, Spaniards) (Phillips 1656: 2, 3…) or, whenever necessary, Catholic rather than Christian (for instance, he spoke of the "Catholick" rather than the Christian faith, 1656: 18). Las Casas criticized those who called themselves Christians, because they behaved inhumanly towards the natives. In fact, he only used the term "católico" three times in his work, whereas "cristiano" is used over a hundred times.

The use of this anti-Spanish and anti-Catholic narrative in Phillips's version in order to boost an English identity had no limits. Even taking Las Casas's words literally, Phillips must have judged the friar insufficiently unequivocal in his depiction of the destruction in the Americas. He omitted, added or adapted his words whenever he deemed appropriate, stretching the fictionalization of the account as he seemed fit. In the following passage Las Casas explicitly mentioned the numbers of people killed in the Hispaniola Island "más de doce cuentos de almas, hombres, mujeres y niños; y en verdad que creo, sin pensar engañarme, que son más de quince cuentos." The unreliability of Las Casas words is shown in the fact that, within the same sentence, he mentions that twelve million men, women and children could have been killed, or perhaps it was fifteen million. This is rendered as "above Twelve millions of souls, women and children being numbred in this sad and fatall lift; moreover I do verily believe that I should speak within compass, should I say that above Fifty millions were consumed in this Massacre", where "hombres" [men] has been omitted and "quince" [fifteen] is turned into "fifty" (no possible justification on the basis of the similarity of the Spanish numerals: "quince" versus "cincuenta").

These accounts contributed decisively to the political agendas of the many pamphleteers of the period, such as Richard Hakluyt, who was to become the ideologue of "English Oceanic enterprise under Elizabeth I" (Garcés 2006: 206). Hakluyt was, indeed, familiar with John Phillips's version of the book, which was to become the masterpiece of this hatred by presenting the translation of his work as a justification to fight against Spain and in favour of the conquest of America by the English (Frohock 2004: 30). As Powell indicates, the relationship between Hakluyt and Theodore De Bry, a Flemish engraver, printer, and bookseller, would give a new impetus to the anti-Spanish construct by introducing an intersemiotic translation of the text to accompany the English version: "In 1598 the De Brys of Frankfurt issued an edition of the Brief Relation with a new twist. The work contained seventeen engravings illustrating specific episodes of purported Spanish torture and killing of Indians (…)" (1971: 80).

Translation contributed to the export of the powerful invention of Spain as an evil nation or a nation of evildoers: "America's impression of Spain was colored by the Black Legend, first popularized by Dutch and English Protestant writers" (Stein 2002: 248). Translations of the tract were produced again in the late years of the nineteenth century when the US needed to build the case for American intervention in Cuba and the Philippines. In 1898 a New York publisher produced *An Historical and True Account of the Cruel Massacre and Slaughter of 20,000,000 People in the West Indies by the Spaniards* (Powell 1971: 122). Hanke recalls that this edition included a blank page with the explanation that "the illustration origi-nally planned to be there was simply too frightful to include!" (Hanke 1951:59).

Apart from Las Casas's English versions, translations of other Spanish wit-nesses of the conquest were also available, including Acosta's *Historia natural y moral de las Indias* (Seville, 1590), translated into English and other European languages. His *De Procuranda Indorum Salute* (or *How to Provide for the Salvation of the Indians*) provided a different perspective on the European presence in the Americas, presenting the challenges for indigenous peoples and Spaniards alike (Mills & Taylor 2006:116). However, it was Las Casas that attracted the attention of the ideologues of the period because he provided the justification for the pre-sentation of Spain as a nation of abominable Catholic monsters and promoted the identity of the English as entitled to liberate the noble savage from the evil con-queror, not the European, not the Christian one, but the Catholic Spaniard. The words of Phillips, as he addresses Oliver Cromwell (not crown prince Phillip) in his dedicatory, leave no doubt. He writes about "Your just anger against the Bloudy and Popish nations of the Spaniards, whose superstitions have exceeded those of Canaan."

Invented Europe or invented Europes?

Las Casas and La Malinche exemplify a very different, if complementary, ver-sion of the role of translation in the conquest of the Americas, in the relation-ship between the Europeans and the Amerindians. The use of historical figures has become an integral part of the process of invention that Rabasa mentioned, and has contributed, through translation and conceptual interpretations of the translational activity, to the promotion of certain narratives of Europe and the Americas, often antagonistic. Thus, the additional role played by translation in the construction of identity in the Americas seems far less positive than in Gentzler's discussion of the fictional turn (2008). Translation is not so much about fidelity, he claims, as it is about embellishments, differences, and digressions (2008:113). Drawing on Borges's approach to and use of translation, the activity itself can be an act of rebellion against European colonial rule (2008:115). As mentioned, this positivized view of translation has also been related to the concept of cannibalism, which has become useful in "allowing access to modes of thought repressed po-litically an intellectually" (Gentzler 2008:79). But, as Gentzler also acknowledges, the term has a double meaning which draws on "European pejorative notions of cannibalism as a barbaric and heretical act" (2008:78).

This second component of the term is, indeed, present in the Las Casas's trans-lations, because, as Vidal has recently pointed out, translation "es una actividad que puede ser tanto de resistencia como de dominación" (2010: 82). 17th century versions of Las Casas's work epitomized the less flattering perception of cannibalism, whereby the writers recreate, reelaborate and rewrite. The fictional turn becomes a fictionalizing twist as translators conflate the worst of the enemy with the worst of themselves in an attempt to promote local (or national) identity at the expense of the Other. Thus, the translational activity influenced the way in which the various nations of Europe chose to interpret their rivals within the European context, closer to Gavronsky's view of translation as violence, as rape (1977, quoted in Chamberlain 1988: 462). It is perhaps in this sense that the concept of Eurocentrism becomes more coherent, when it is considered from the perspective of anti-Eurocentrism, from outside Europe itself.

Otherwise, we should talk about a plurality of concepts associated with Europe. To speak of identity in Europe was and still remains wishful thinking: the many national identities, even within the nation-states, allow us to speak of the many Europes of the past and the present. And we are talking about a present where attempts at promoting a European identity have been less than successful (Delanty 1995: 128), and where the existence of Europe (let alone Eurocentrism) is questioned on a daily basis even by international economic and political figures who fall prey to the temptation of blaming Europe's multiculturalism and multilingualism for its current economic concerns.[3] For this reason, I would like to conclude by retrieving Rabasa's discussion on the invention of America, where he called for a new universal plurality derived from "the possibility of reinventing the world from a non-European perspective" (2003: 18). I suggest that there is a need to re-examine the concept of Eurocentrism itself as well as the contradictions and complexities of identity in the so-called Old Continent. And the various layers of translation studies and the translational activity need to be reassessed to include the less positive elements that characterize a fictionalizing twist that draws on the worst of the source and target texts and cultures. This reassessment would certainly contribute to the recognition of the diversity, if not the difference, existing in the West, which Bhabha had already mentioned as a key element to understanding the relations between empires and colonies (1994: 35–36).

---

3. Nobel Prize winner Paul Krugman has recently voiced his explanation for the current economic and political troubles of Europe thus: "America, we know, has a currency union that works, and we know why it works: because it coincides with a nation — a nation with a big central government, a common language and a shared culture." Published in *The New York Times* on 01/16/2011 and translated and posted on the same day by Spain's *El Pais*, for example.

References

Alarcón, Norma. 2006. "Traduttora, traditora: una figura paradigmática del feminismo de las chicanas." In *Fronteras y cruces: cartografía de escenarios culturales latinoamericanos,* edited by Marisa Belausteguigoitia and Martha Leñero, 123–152. México: UNAM.

Adorno, Rolena. 2002. "Washington Irving's Romantic Hispanism and Its Columbian Legacies." In *Spain in America. The Origins of Hispanism in the United States,* edited by Richard L. Kagan, 49–105. Urbana/Chicago: University of Illinois Press.

Aranda, Lucía V. 2007. *Handbook of Spanish-English Translation.* Lanham, Maryland: University Press of America.

Arrojo, Rosemary. 1999. "Interpretative as Possessive Love. Hélène Cixous, Clarice Lispector and the Ambivalence of Fidelity." In *Post-colonial Translation. Theory and Practice* edited by Susan Bassnett and Harish Trivedi, 141–161. London/New York: Routledge.

Baker, Mona and Saldanha, Gabriela (eds). 2009. *Routledge Encyclopedia of Translation Studies.* London/New York: Routledge.

Bassnett, Susan and Harish Trivedi. 1999. "Introduction: Of Colonies, Cannibals and Vernaculars." In *Post-colonial Translation. Theory and Practice,* edited by Susan Bassnett and Harish Trivedi, 1–18. London/New York: Routledge.

Bassnett, Susan. 2010. "Postcolonial Translations." In *A Concise Companion to Postcolonial Literature,* edited by Shirley Chew and David Richards, 78–96. Chichester: Wiley-Blackwell.

Belausteguigoitia, Marisa and Martha Leñero (eds). 2006. *Fronteras y cruces: cartografía de escenarios culturales latinoamericanos.* México: UNAM.

Bhabha, Homi. 1994. *The Location of Culture.* London/New York: Routledge.

Brinton, Andrea K. 2009. *Shaping British Identity: Transatlantic Anglo-Spanish Rivalry in the Early Modern Period.* Ph Thesis. The University of Texas at Arlington.

Casas, Bartolomé de las. 2009. *Brevísima relación de la destrucción de las Indias.* Barcelona: Linkgua.

Chamberlain, Lori. 1988. "Gender and the Metaphorics of Translation." *Signs: Journal of Women in Culture and Society* 13.3: 454–472.

Corpi, Lucha. 2001. *Palabras de mediodía/Noon words.* Translated by Catherine Rodríguez-Nieto. Houston: University of Houston.

Damrosch, David. 2003. *What is World Literature?* Princeton/Oxford: Princeton University Press.

Delabastita, Dirk. 2009. "Fictional Representations." In *Routledge Encyclopedia of Translation Studies,* edited by Mona Baker and Gabriela Saldanha, 109–111. London/New York: Routledge.

Delanty, Gerard. 1995. *Inventing Europe. Idea, Identity, Reality.* New York: Palgrave.

———. 2006. "Modernity and the Escape from Eurocentrism". In *Handbook of Contemporary European Social Theory,* edited by Gerard Delanty, 266–278. London/New York: Routledge.

Díaz, Bernal. 1963. *The Conquest of New Spain.* Translated by J. M. Cohen. Harmondsworth: Penguin.

Domingues, José Maurício. 2006. "Social theory, 'Latin' America and modernity." In *Handbook of Contemporary European Social Theory,* edited by Gerard Delanty, 381–393. London: New York: Routledge.

———. 2008. *Latin America and Contemporary Modernity. A Sociological Interpretation.* London/New York: Routledge.

Donovan, Bill M. 1992. *Introduction to The Devastation of the Indies. A Brief Account*. Baltimore: The John Hopkins University Press.

Frohock, Richard. 2004. *Heroes of Empire: the British Imperial Protagonist in America, 1596–1764*. Cranbury, NJ: University of Delaware Press.

Garcés, María Antonia. 2006. "The Translator Translated: Inca Garcilaso and English Imperial Expansion." In *Travel and Translation in the Early Modern Period*, edited by Carmine G. Di Biase, 203–225. Amsterdam: Rodopi.

Gentzler, Edwin. 2008. *Translation and Identity in the Americas: New Directions in Translation Theory*. London and New York: Routledge.

Green, John R. 1895. *A Short History of the English People*. London/New York: MacMillan.

González Hernández, Cristina. 2002. *Doña Marina (La Malinche) y la formación de la identidad mexicana*. Madrid: Ediciones Encuentro.

Hanke, Lewis. 1951. *Bartolomé de las Casas: an Interpretation of His Life and Writings*. The Hague: Nijhoff.

Harris, Olivia. 2006. "The Coming of the White People. Reflections on the Mythologization of History in Latin America." In *Colonial Spanish America. A Documentary Story*, edited by Kenneth R. Mills and William B. Taylor, 34–45. Oxford: SR Books.

Kagan, Richard L., ed. 2002. *Spain in America. The Origins of Hispanism in the United States*. Urbana/Chicago: University of Illinois Press.

Kamen, Henry. 2001. "Vicissitudes of a World Power 1500–1700." In *Spain. A History*, edited by Raymond Carr, 152–172. Oxford: Oxford University Press.

Larkosh, Christopher. 2004. "Levinas, Latin American Thought and the Futures of Translational Ethics." *TTR: Traduction, terminologie, rédaction* 17.2:27–44.

Lefevere, André. 1995. "Translators and the Reins of Power". In *Translators through History*, edited by Jean Delisle and Judith Woodsworth, 131–158. Amsterdam/New York: John Benjamins.

Mills, Kenneth R. and William B. Taylor (eds). 2006. *Colonial Spanish America. A Documentary Story*. Oxford: SR Books.

Milton, John and Paul Bandia. 2009. "Introduction: Agents of Translation and Translation Studies." In *Agents of Translation*,[4] edited by John Milton and Paul F. Bandia, 1–18. Amsterdam/New York: John Benjamins.

Moreiras, Alberto. 1999. *Tercer espacio: literatura y duelo en América Latina*. Santiago: Lom Ediciones.

———. 2001. *The Exhaustion of Difference: The Politics of Latin American Cultural Studies*. Durham, North Carolina: Duke University Press.

Munday, Jeremy. 2001. *Introducing Translation Studies*. London/New York: Routledge.

Núñez, Fernanda. 2006. "Malinche." *Fronteras y cruces: cartografía de escenarios culturales latinoamericano*, edited by Marisa Belausteguigoitia and Martha Leñero, 153–162. México: UNAM.

O'Gorman, Edmundo. 2003 (1958). *La invención de América*. México: Fondo de Cultura Económica.

Paz, Octavio. 1997. *El laberinto de la soledad y otras obras*. Hardmonsworth: Penguin.

Phillips, John. 1656. *The Tears of the Indians*. London: Nath Brook.

Pincus, Steven, C. A. 1996. *Protestantism and Patriotism. Ideologies and the Making of English Foreign Policy, 1650–1668*. Cambridge: Cambridge University Press.

Powell, Philip W. 1971. *Tree of Hate, Propaganda Affecting United States Relations with the Hispanic World*. The University of New Mexico Press.

Rabasa, José. 1993. *Inventing America: Spanish Historiography and the Formation of Eurocentrism.* The University of Oklahoma Press.

Restall, Matthew. 2003. *Seven Myths of the Spanish Conquest.* Oxford: Oxford University Press.

Socolow, Susan M. 2000. *The Women of Colonial Latin America.* Oxford: Oxford University Press.

Simon, Sherry. 1996. *Gender in Translation: Cultural Identity and the Politics of Transmission.* London/New York: Routledge.

Snell-Hornby, Mary. 2006. *The Turns of Translation Studies.* Amsterdam/New York: John Benjamins.

Stannard, David E. 1992. *American Holocaust: The Conquest of the New World.* Oxford/New York: Oxford University Press.

Stein, Louise K. 2002. "Before the Latin Tinge: Spanish Music and the "Spanish Idiom" in the United States, 1778–1940." In *Spain in America: The Origins of Hispanism in the United Stated,* edited by Richard L. Kagan, 143–246. Urbana/Chicago: University of Illinois Press.

Sten, Maria. 2003. *Cuando Orestes muere en Veracruz.* México: Fondo de Cultura Económica.

Szurmuk, Mónica and Robert McKee. 2009. *Diccionario de Estudios Culturales Latinoamericanos.* México: Siglo XXI Editores.

Thomas, Hugh. 1993. *Conquest: Cortes, Montezuma and the Fall of Old Mexico.* New York: Touchstone.

Todorov, Tzvetan. 1999. *The Conquest of America: the Question of the Other.* Translated by Richard Howard. Norman, OK: University of Oklahoma Press.

Vidal, Africa. 2010. *Traducción y asimetria.* Frankfurt am Main: Peter Lang.

Zúñiga, Rosa M. 2003. *Malinche, esa ausente siempre presente.* México D. F.: Planeta & Janés.

Zinn, Howard. 2003. *A People's History of the United States.* New York: HarperCollins.

(More than) American prisms on Eurocentrisms

An interview article

Luc van Doorslaer

As was already indicated in the introduction to this volume, we had never expected that a one-day conference would trigger such a lively and highly interesting discussion about Eurocentrism and related views and concepts. After having made the selection of the contributions for this volume and having read the critiques of mainly European authors, we believed it would make sense to establish a balance. Edwin Gentzler's 'American' book served as the impetus for several European and one African author to contribute to this volume. In their well-founded scholarly articles some of them criticize certain approaches quite fundamentally. Although categorization in terms of continents or even a divide is exactly the opposite of what we would like to achieve with this discussion, we cannot ignore the criticism put forward by several European authors regarding aspects of an 'American' view on translation and translation studies. Therefore, we decided to establish the continental balance within this volume by presenting the main 'European' criticisms to a few leading translation studies scholars in the Americas. We asked them to what extent they could agree with some of the criticisms formulated and to comment on them. The three scholars 'interviewed' for this article are Sherry Simon (Concordia University, Montreal), Judy Wakabayashi (Kent State University) and Maria Tymoczko (a colleague of Edwin Gentzler at the University of Massachusetts, Amherst). Each scholar was presented with three sets of questions containing the main points of critique formulated in several of the articles in this volume. Interestingly in their answers the three scholars clearly and explicitly wanted to go beyond their American affiliations. Simon refers to her recent research on Central Europe, Wakabayashi, an Australian, extends the discussion to the Eastern hemisphere (with references to Asia and Australia), Tymoczko describes herself as a "Europeanist by training".

It was the original intention to present the sets of questions to the three scholars and construct the interview article along the lines of those questions. However, Maria Tymoczko explicitly requested that her reflections be published as a single piece, a sort of response paper in the tradition of "the Chesterman/ Arrojo exchange some years ago" in *Target* (starting with Chesterman & Arrojo 2000, followed by a whole series of reactions and responses by several authors, and concluded by Chesterman 2002). Since Tymoczko is probably the author in our discipline who has written about and analyzed the term 'Eurocentrism' the most over the last few years (in several publications), we agreed to her request. The first part of this article will deal with the answers given by Simon and Wakabayashi, whereas Tymoczko's reflections are published as a whole in the last part. It goes without saying that we would like to thank the three colleagues for their kind and stimulating collaboration for this interview article.

Translation in the American sense?

Almost all the authors contributing to this volume praise Edwin Gentzler's book, *Translation and Identity in the Americas,* for its wide scope and fascinating material. At the same time they have the impression that "translation in the American sense" feels like a construction partly based on "counter-European self affirmation" and sometimes overextending (pan-American) identity claims. We asked the interviewees to comment on this on the basis of their own experience as translation scholars in the Americas. Wakabayashi (an Australian) chose not to comment on this first topic because her field of specialization is not translation in the Americas.

Simon writes: "I am not certain that I understand this critique. It seems to me that the history of migration to the Americas and subsequent growth of settler colonies, their violence against indigenous communities, and the interaction between dominant colonial powers and other immigrant groups — all these factors contribute to a history which is different from that of Europe and which therefore demands its own frames of reference. Now, interestingly, I have recently become interested in the ways that the history of Central Europe (the Habsburg lands and beyond) are treated as a model of 'postcolonialism'. Europe too had its colonization of the East, and this colonization resulted in the multilingual societies of Central Europe — a multilingualism which came to a violent end with World War II. So one could see certain broad similarities and write histories which might invoke similar kinds of translational histories. On the other hand, the histories of Western Europe again are very different, because these countries have only now (since the 1980s or so) become countries of in-migration rather than out-migration. What is fascinating in Gentzler's book is that translation can serve as a key to understanding cultural history. Whether this is an American or a European cultural history (each of which must be understood in its own terms and according to its own specific patterns of settlement and intermixture), it remains that translation is a valuable — indeed essential — conceptual prism to adopt for exploration."

Both geographical and mental constructs

A second set of questions referred to a tendency in translation studies identified by some of the authors which involves replacing the old nationalist (linguistic) categories by a "continent-based paradigm" or a "continentalization of discourse": translation studies in the Americas, in Africa, in Asia. We asked the interviewees what their opinion is on the use of geographically based terms to describe developments in a worldwide discipline. Did they think that translation studies might run the risk of over-generalization by using these terms, i.e., by possibly ignoring contradictions and complexities within each continent?

Wakabayashi remarks: "It is essential to note that such labels are not just geographical markers — they are also mental constructs. For instance, the fluid and fuzzy term 'Asia' was devised in the West (initially to refer to Anatolia or the Persian empire), and until contact with Europeans this concept did not exist in the region to which it now refers, because the peoples there did not conceive of themselves as part of a connected entity, although today 'Asia' is increasingly becoming a self-constructing concept. Importantly, it also refers to the imaginary mental space that denotes the West's 'Other', while Gunaratne argues, 'the West connotes all those who evince allegiance to the Eurocentric worldview (including Western-trained non-Western scholars who eagerly advance European universalism for their scholarly productivity), and the East connotes all those who see merit in the Oriental worldview (including Western scholars who strive to replace Eurocentrism with universal universalism)' (2009: 376).

With growing scholarly interconnectedness, such putative categories are becoming more porous. Today the West is an inextricable part of the 'non-West' (another problematic term that takes the West as the matrix and portrays 'the Rest' as a lack, an absence of Westernness) — even though the reverse does not hold true to the same extent. Yet although such questions of terminology are significant, far more important are the realities — i.e., the fact that translation studies today remains dominated by a relatively narrow worldview, being skewed toward Western European and Northern American experiences and understandings, although this is slowly starting to change."

Simon notes that this reframing of translation studies is related to the growth of the discipline on other continents: "The work on translation studies in other parts of the world is an absolutely necessary corrective to European-centered models of translation. Many excellent works have been produced in the last decade on translation in Asia, Africa, and Latin America. But what theorists have seen is that changing geographical sites is not sufficient of course: translation activities in other historical or geographical contexts must be understood in the terms of their own histories and conceptualizations. Do I worry that translation will overextend its reach and become 'n'importe quoi'? No. Translation is showing itself to be an extremely valuable perspective from which to rewrite the histories of cultural encounters and interactions — and to track these histories into ever new sites and venues."

Smaller instead of larger units?

The risk of over-generalization in using continent-based terms is confirmed by Wakabayashi: "Replacing nation-based constructs with region- or continent-based categories does risk compounding the existing neglect of internal diversity and translation cultures that extend across geopolitical borders." Both scholars prefer to turn to smaller and more local units to avoid that risk. Simon: "I have recently turned to the city as another kind of paradigm which undercuts the model of the nation (my book on Montreal and my forthcoming book on other cities in translation). And so rather than extending the geographical reach, moving into larger and larger territories, I have looked to a smaller unit — looking for the kind of richness in the 'local' that Michael Cronin talks about. My aims in engaging in this research were, however, I think very similar to those that Gentzler has taken on in his work on the Americas and which try to move away from using the nation as the default border of analysis and conceptualization. In Gentzler's case, the aim was clearly to show the United States as part of the Americas and therefore not to use the borders of the country as a way of reinforcing an isolationist history. My aim was also to show how language-consciousness pervades city life, and to argue in favor of contact and mixing. For both Gentzler and myself, this means challenging some of the normative models of translation studies itself and to propose a broader meaning for translation."

Wakabayashi also prefers to use categories other than nation- or continent-based ones, although she realizes that the use of such categories cannot always be avoided: "In that sense, it is more valid to focus on local spaces (defined in an ad-hoc manner based on conditions 'on the ground') and the personal, textual and intellectual networks that connect them to other configurations, including those that extend well beyond local contact zones. These might include cultural units such as Chinese-reading Asia (i.e., China, Japan, Korea and Vietnam), defined not along geographical or ethnic fault lines but, for instance, by their shared use of a language and script and a shared literary canon. Nevertheless, the use of reductionist labels based on geographical regions or pseudo-geographic designations such as 'the West' is a shorthand expedient that is perhaps unavoidable to some extent. Moreover, terms such as 'Africa' function as a reminder of how vast swathes of the world (not just internal differences) remain understudied, simply falling off the map for most translation scholars, although researchers within these regions are surely aware of the historical and cultural hybridity, as well as differences in translation thinking and practice."

About terminology and ideology

The last set of questions focused on the central theme of this volume, the concept of 'Eurocentrism', and was inextricably linked to the reflections of the second question. We put forward the hypothesis to the interviewees that there seemed to be a certain terminological fuzziness regarding the terms 'Eurocentric', 'Western' and 'European', and their relationship to each other. We asked them how they understood the relationship between these terms, and to what extent they would agree with the authors who experience "anti-Eurocentrism as a convenient concept to promote a certain sense of unity, of uniformity" or who experience Euro-centric images as "metaphors and metonyms for regimes of dominance and oppression"?

Wakabayashi: "These terms conceal more than they reveal. 'Western' is usually regarded as largely synonymous with the discursive constructs 'Europe' and 'America', thereby ignoring not only 'Western' nations in other parts of the world, such as Australia and New Zealand, but also overlooking internal differences (e.g., Eastern Europe, Canada). Eurocentrism is a mindset that is linked to but goes beyond these ostensibly geographic terms. In that sense, it does entail 'dominance and oppression', but more as a result of unthinking ignorance rather than deliberate intellectual imperialism. The fact that some European scholars have reservations about anti-Eurocentric arguments is understandable (although still problematic), as the frog-in-a-well syndrome means it is always harder to see oneself objectively than it is for an outsider gazing in. Challenging Eurocentrism does not mean replacing it with Americacentrism, for instance. *Rejecting* Eurocentric or Western thinking outright risks falling into the same binary trap or ending up in an intellectual ghetto; *critiquing* the West runs risks such as self-orientalizing; and *adapting* Western concepts still means working within the Western paradigm. What is needed is to dislocate such polarizations and the unequal relations they represent — and a terminology that allows this. How can we think about translation outside Europe and, more broadly, outside the West in ways that are more grounded in local contexts and epistemology yet also complement and engage with insights from contemporary thinking in the West, while helping to free it from its current confines? The first step is greater openness and sensitiveness to non-Euro-American views and modes of translation, to local specificities, aesthetics and values, to different concepts of genre and different concepts of textual (trans)formation. A rhizometric approach that emphasizes multiple entry points can foster receptiveness to more pluralistic understandings of translation without marginalizing or homogenizing them. Particularly interesting would be a greater focus on horizontal South-South interactions (e.g., an Arab-Latin American axis), as these do not conform to the usual 'center–periphery' hierarchies."

Simon sees the historical value of the term 'Euro-centric', but is aware of the ideological aspect that cannot be avoided: "Terminology always carries its own ideological agenda. The debates over the meaning of Europe and particularly of the idea of Eastern Europe — debates initiated most famously by Milan Kundera and extending today to the scholars who now work on Central Europe–refusing the idea of East or West and most emphatically refusing the nostalgia of *Mitteleuropa* — these debates show how embattled the idea of Europe is. And of course no one showed more clearly what the idea of the West entailed than Edward Said in his exploration of the West's opposite: the Orient. Euro-centric is a useful term, however, to expose the 'naturalism' of preexisting models of thought, the ideas one takes for granted. Maria Tymoczko has been particularly effective in exposing the limits of the ideas which have been taken for granted in translation studies."

Tymoczko's position paper

This reference is the perfect transition to Maria Tymoczko's position paper on this topic. She had received the same sets of questions as the other scholars, but preferred to answer in one piece "that takes shape within a somewhat larger coherent framework that does not entail the problematic assumptions behind the questions asked in the interview." We here publish the rest of her answer unabridged and unchanged:

"In translation studies and other fields, there is a significant problem with terminology in discussing epistemic filiation and dominance in discourse. As many scholars have pointed out — particularly those from Asian traditions, the Arab world, and Turkic cultures — at present one cannot productively use the term 'Western' to clearly delineate any culture or to sort out cultural discourses. For one thing, the contrast Western/Eastern brings with it the shadow of Orientalism. Moreover, the dichotomy implicitly presupposes a particular perspective and an assumed cultural center. For example, if China rather than Europe is taken as 'the middle kingdom' — as Chinese culture considered itself for many centuries — then the Americas are obviously part of 'the East'. More importantly, there has been extensive cultural interchange in the last century such that many, indeed most, modern cultures around the world have become 'Westernized', sharing similar signature 'Western' cultural features including a common technology, common features of material culture, and common bodies of knowledge. From this standpoint, arguably Japan is probably the most 'Westernized' culture in the world.

At the same time most scholars acknowledge that we have arrived at these widely shared cultural patterns from very different starting points. One sees those differences clearly in comparing the large blocks of affiliated cultures — European cultures vs. those of the Chinese culture area; Turkic cultures vs. the diverse Indo-European and Dravidian cultures of India; the diverse cultures of the Arab world vs. the many cultures of Africa; and of course the native cultures of the Americas, Australia, and the diverse islands of the world from those of Indonesia to New Zealand and Hawaii. In turn these culture areas are normally differentiated at even greater levels of delicacy by their specific languages, cultural practices, histories, and the like. We need terms that allow us to speak about this vast diversity of cultural frameworks and to distinguish them from the dominant epistemic frameworks that have spread throughout the world since the age of European imperialism and that have consolidated their hold since globalization. (Note that in speaking thus of recent world history, I am not demonizing Europe: at its height China similarly dominated its culture area epistemically and the same pattern was also characteristic of most other early imperial networks.)

In speaking about the need for broadening the epistemic purview of translation studies, I (and many others) have adopted the term 'Eurocentric' to talk about the problematic dominance in this academic field of ideas and perspectives that have European roots and European presuppositions, with a consequent exclusion of other world perspectives. But the term 'Eurocentric' is not the same as 'European' and does not imply the "continentalization" of discourse about translation studies. As the term 'Eurocentrism' is generally used, the dominant cultures of the Americas and Australia are Eurocentric, because the dominant cultures of those continents use European languages and share their major cultural concepts and tenets with Europe. The dominant cultures in the Americas and Australia are rooted in European history, European textual traditions, and European intellectual history, among other things.

If we examine translation studies as it has developed thus far, we see that although there are both differences and similarities between, say, translation traditions in Germany and France, or Ireland and England, nonetheless these particular differences and similarities are subsumed within parameters that are common to the larger culture area of Europe. When we turn to the Americas, it is equally clear that there are differences in the translation patterns among the various nations and that there are similarities across the Americas resulting from their shared geopolitical position, their common histories as European colonies, and other factors including their status as immigrant nations. Nonetheless, both the differences and commonalities in the Americas with regard to translation per se are in turn subsumed within larger intellectual and cultural frameworks shared with the nations of Europe. That is, the countries of the Americas are Eurocentric even though not European.

The reason to talk about Eurocentrism in translation studies is that at present there are a number of different strands being developed in the field that all tend toward broadening the discipline beyond the presuppositions about translation rooted in European languages and the cultures and histories of Eurocentric nations. Most of these strands do not contrast the Americas with Europe, nor are they intent on 'continentalizing' discourses about translation. It seems obvious to myself and to many other scholars in the field that translation studies can only be strengthened if there is more discourse from and about China, other east Asian nations, southeast Asia, India, Turkic cultures, the Arab world, and so forth, not to mention the native cultures of Africa, the Americas, Australia, Polynesia, and other places. Within these studies, there is obviously a place for the study of any national tradition of translation or translation theorization, hence Chinese translation studies as well as Belgian translation studies. Such broadening of the field will strengthen translation theory and will make translation practices more flexible, both of which are imperatives at present if the field is to meet the challenges of new technologies and a globalizing world.

I find that such broadening and deepening of the field are particularly urgent at present in order to counter the contemporary semiotic and epistemic narrowing associated with the dominance of global English. At present I also perceive a specific tendency toward narrowing concerns about translation in Europe that can be attributed to the preoccupation of many European translation scholars with the current needs of the E.U. for translators who are specifically prepared to operate within models promulgated by the European Union and required by the European Commission. The funding of many European research programs about translation by the E.U. is also slanting European scholarship in translation studies in directions focused on the needs of the E.U. These latter comments of mine obviously lead to whole realms that are controversial, that need extensive scholarly discussion, and that I cannot elaborate upon in this context. They should nonetheless be obvious upon reflection.

Insofar as there is a continentalization of translation studies, it is and has been European continentalization. It can be hard for Europeans to perceive this implicit state of the discipline, but European continentalization is explicitly written into the first four decades of the scholarship of the field, beginning with the 1959 landmark collection in which the signature articles by Jakobson and Quine appeared. For the next 40 years, almost all the exemplification of translation history in descriptive studies and in formulations of translation theory was based on European data and European presuppositions about translation inherent in the very terminology used. The principal deviations from this pattern have been found in the work of the theorists of Bible translation, notably Eugene Nida; in materials written in non-European languages (such as Chinese and Japanese); and in studies written in European languages that have been largely confined to a local readership (such as studies in Brazilian Portuguese). Meanwhile, with the rise of global English and globalization in general, translation studies has become a thriving enterprise in Asia, Latin America, the Arab world, Turkic cultures, and around the globe. Discourses about Eurocentrism are one tool being used to decenter the field, to open up translation theory to broader perspectives, to enlarge exemplification, and to break the boundaries constraining the epistemology of translation studies as it has developed within the implicit European continentalization that has characterized the field for most of its history."

To conclude

In her accompanying email, Maria Tymoczko writes that the main goal of her scholarship is "to have interesting and productive dialogue about translation throughout the world, rather than trying to corral academic capital, increase prestige, grind old axes, fan rivalries, or whatever." We wholeheartedly support this approach and hope that this interview article may serve as an illustration. Moreover, we hope that the reflections of the three scholars may serve as a stepping stone for the further exchange of ideas and responses — in line with the best possible academic tradition.

References

Chesterman, Andrew and Rosemary Arrojo. 2000. "Shared Ground in Translation Studies." *Target* 12.1:151–160.

Chesterman, Andrew. 2002. "Shared Ground Revisited." *Target* 14.1:143–148.

Gunaratne, Shelton A. 2009. "Emerging Global Divides in Media and Communication Theory: European Universalism versus Non-Western Reactions." *Asian Journal of Communication* 19.4:366–383.

Notes on contributors

Michael Boyden (1977) is Assistant Professor of American Culture at Ghent University College. He has studied at the University of Leuven, Queens University Belfast, the University of British Columbia and Harvard University. He is the author of *Predicting the Past: The Paradoxes of American Literary History* (2009). He has published articles on American literature, translation theory and literary multilingualism. Current work involves the multilingual testimonies of immigrants who went to the US through the port of Antwerp during the period 1870–1945.

Dirk Delabastita is Professor of English Literature and Literary Theory at the University of Namur and Research Fellow at K.U. Leuven, where he is a member of the CETRA staff. He wrote his PhD on Shakespeare's wordplay in *Hamlet* and the problems of translating it (*There's a Double Tongue*, published in 1993). He edited two further volumes on the translation of wordplay: *Wordplay and Translation* (1996, special issue of *The Translator*) and *Traductio. Essays on Punning and Translation* (1997). Dirk Delabastita also co-authored a Dutch-language dictionary of literary terms (*Lexicon van Literaire Termen*, with Hendrik van Gorp and Rita Ghesquiere, seventh edition, 2007). His other books include *European Shakespeares* (edited with Lieven D'hulst, 1993), *Fictionalizing Translation and Multilingualism* (special issue of *Linguistica Antverpiensia*, edited with Rainier Grutman, 2005) and *Shakespeare and European Politics* (edited with Jozef de Vos and Paul Franssen, 2008). He belongs to the editorial board of *The Translator*.

Peter Flynn is an associate professor in Translation Studies and English at the University of Leuven (Antwerp Campus) and is also a member of the CETRA staff. He completed a PhD in Language and Literature at Ghent University where he worked as a lecturer in the English Department from 1999 to 2006. His dissertation comprises a linguistic ethnographic study of literary translation practices among translators in the Netherlands and Flanders, as well as a corpus study of (English-language) Irish poetry in Dutch translation. He has published in *Perspectives, Target, Text and Talk,* and *The Handbook of Translation Studies.* Prior to this, he worked as a self-employed professional translator and has continued to translate on a regular basis since. His main areas of interest include: ethnographies of translation practices, empirical and functionalist approaches to translation studies, translation theory, (linguistic) ethnography, (Irish) literature, and sociolinguistics.

Edwin Gentzler is Professor of Comparative Literature and Director of the Translation Center at the University of Massachusetts, Amherst. He is the author of *Translation and Identity in the Americas: New Directions in Translation Theory* (Routledge, 2008) and *Contemporary Translation Theories* (Routledge, 1993), which has been issued in two revised versions (Multilingual Matters, 2001 and Shanghai Foreign Language Education Press, 2003) and translated into Portuguese, Italian, Bulgarian, Arabic, and Persian. He is the co-editor (with Maria Tymoczko) of *Translation and Power* (Amherst: University of Massachusetts Press, 2002) and serves as co-editor (with Susan Bassnett) of the Topics in Translation Series for Multilingual Matters, as well as an executive committee member of the American Translation and Interpreting Studies Association (ATISA).

Kobus Marais holds a Ph.D. in Ancient Near Eastern literature, a Master's Degree in Translation Studies, and a Baccalaureate Degree in Theology. He joined the University of the Free State in Bloemfontein (South Africa) in July 2006 as Senior Lecturer. He teaches translation theory and practice and text theory at the undergraduate and postgraduate level. He is also involved in community service learning. His research interests include translator education, complexity theory and its implications for translation; he is currently embarking on research on translation and development.

Roberto A. Valdeón was awarded a Master's degree in English Literature and Translation Studies from the University of Glasgow (1988), and obtained his Ph.D. in English Studies from the University of Oviedo (1993). He has published extensively on EFL and translation, including contributions to *Perspectives*, *Across Languages and Cultures*, *Meta*, *Linguistica Antverpiensia*, *Target*, *International Journal of Applied Linguistics*, *Babel*, *Forum*, *The Translator*, *Languages in Contrast*, *Phrasis* and *Trans*. He is a member of the international advisory board of *Vigo International Journal of Applied Linguistics* (University of Vigo) and John Benjamins' *Handbook of Translation Studies*. He is also a co-editor of *Perspectives* and was the chairman of an international conference on "Translation in the Era of Information" (October 2008). He is the editor of *Translating Information* (2010) and has guest-edited special issues of *Vigo International Journal of Applied Linguistics*, *Perspectives* and *Across Languages and Cultures*. As a member of Aedean (the Spanish Association for Anglo-American Studies), he chairs the Translation Studies section. He will join the faculty at the University of Massachusetts Amherst as a visiting professor in 2011–12.

Luc van Doorslaer is an Associate Professor in Translation and Journalism Studies as well as Vice-Dean for Research at the University of Leuven – Campus Antwerp (Belgium). As a Research Fellow he is affiliated with Stellenbosch University (South Africa). He is a staff member of CETRA, the Centre for Translation Studies (KU Leuven). Together with Yves Gambier, he is the editor of the online *Translation Studies Bibliography* (9th release 2012) and the volumes of the new *Handbook of Translation Studies* (2010-ongoing). His main research interests are: ideology and translation, journalism and translation, imagology and translation, Translation Studies resources. He also works as a journalist for Dutch-language Belgian television.

Name index

Subject index